FROM SICKERT TO GERTLER

MODERN BRITISH ART FROM BOXTED HOUSE

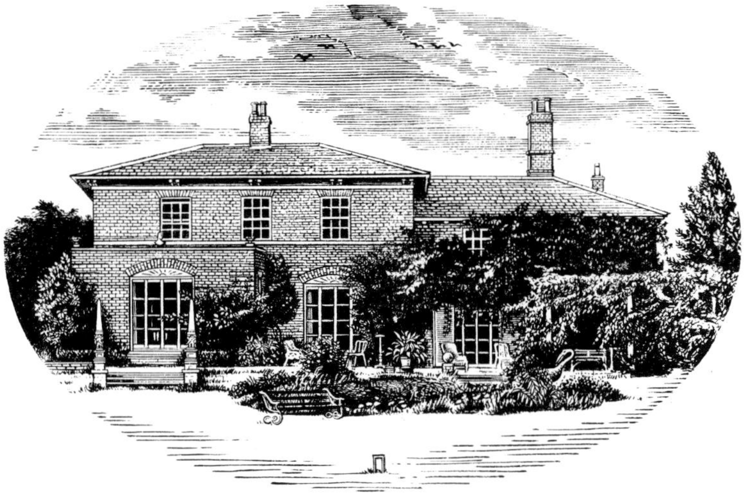

DEDICATED TO THE MEMORY OF

NATALIE BEVAN 1909–2007

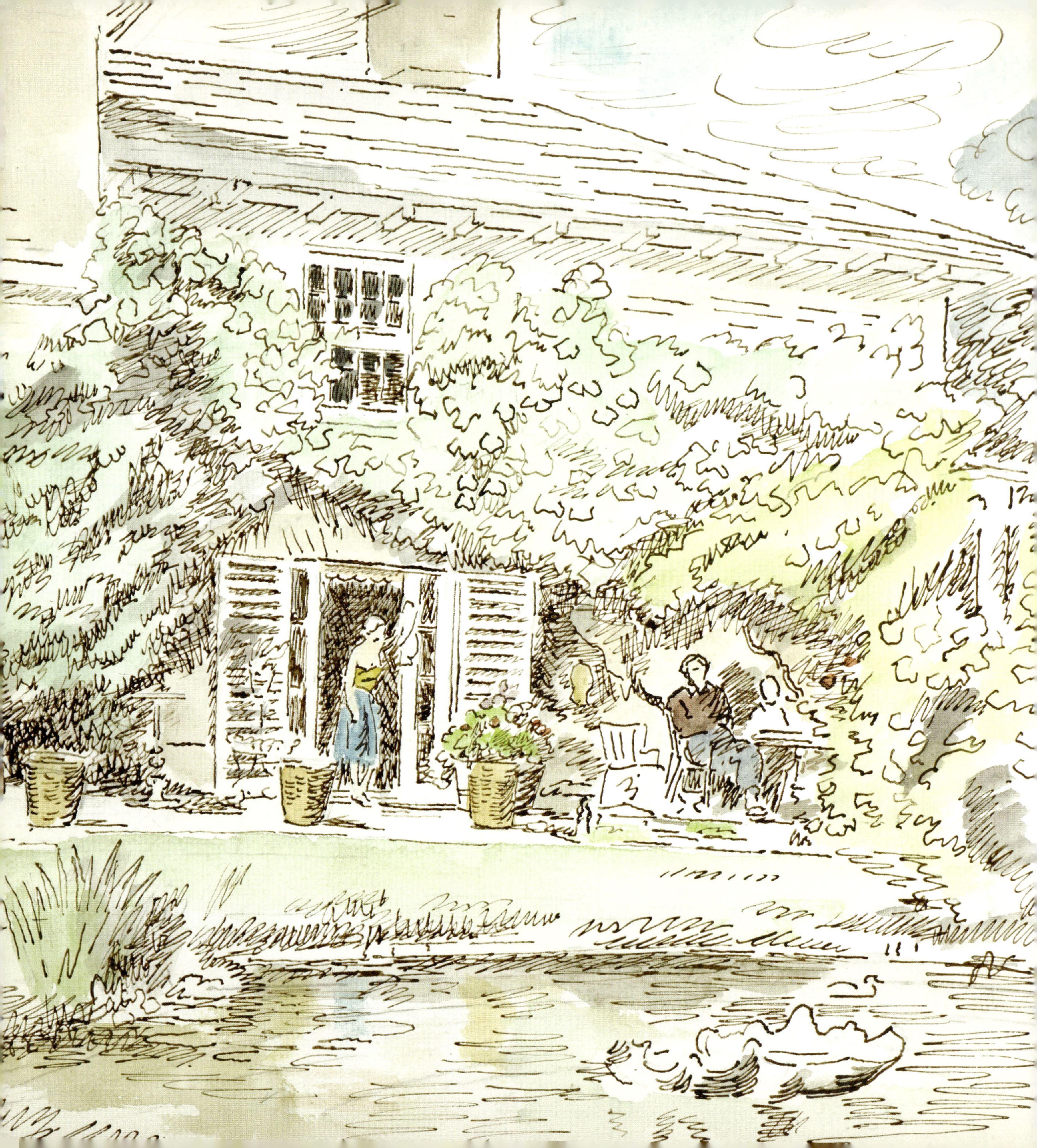

From Sickert to Gertler
Modern British Art from Boxted House

Alice Strang
with contributions from Frances Stenlake, Caroline Cuthbert & Dick Chapman

National Galleries of Scotland · 2008

Published by the Trustees of the National Galleries of Scotland to accompany the exhibition, *From Sickert to Gertler: Modern British Art from Boxted House*, held at the Scottish National Gallery of Modern Art, Edinburgh, from 15 March 2008 to 22 June 2008. A reduced version will be shown at Gainsborough's House, Sudbury from 4 October to 13 December 2008.

ISBN 978 1 906270 06 3

Designed and typeset in Custodia by Dalrymple
Printed on Hello Matt 170gsm by Nicholson & Bass, Northern Ireland

Front cover: Mark Gertler, detail from *Supper (Natalie Denny)*, *1928*, private collection
Back cover: *Library*, *Boxted House*,
Photograph by Thomas Stewart
Half-title: Denzil Reeves, *Boxted House*, *c.*1958,
Private collection
Frontispiece: Adrian Daintrey, detail from *Natalie and Bobby on the Terrace*, *Boxted House*, 1957
Private collection

The proceeds from the sale of this book go towards supporting the National Galleries of Scotland.

www.nationalgalleries.org

Foreword

THIS book and the exhibition at the Scottish National Gallery of Modern Art, which it accompanies, celebrate the fine art which hung in Boxted House, the Essex home of Bobby and Natalie Bevan from 1947 until Bobby's death in 1974. The art consisted of works by Bobby's parents, the painters Robert Pohill Bevan and Stanislawa de Karlowska and their circle, and by artists whom Bobby and Natalie met in London in the 1920s before their marriage, which included Christopher Nevinson and John Armstrong, and by friends who were based in East Anglia after World War Two, such as John Nash and Cedric Morris. Needless to say, the Bevans' collection was always evolving, as they also acquired works in other fields, and its display changed over time as they bought, sold and lent works to galleries all over Britain. However, the exhibition and book focus on the collection as it was on Natalie's death in 2007 and on the modern British highlights.

This is the third time that art from Boxted has been shown in a public gallery, following the Minories art gallery, Colchester in 1975 and Gainsborough's House, Sudbury in 1978. We are delighted that highlights of the Edinburgh exhibition will return to Gainsborough's House thirty years later, and during their fiftieth anniversary year. It has been a pleasure working on this tour with Diane Perkins and her team.

This project continues the Scottish National Gallery of Modern Art's commitment to showing private collections, which, thanks to the generosity of our lenders, allows the public to see works usually hidden away from view. As such, it reflects Bobby and Natalie's own philanthropy as patrons of the arts and recalls past exhibitions of work acquired by Gabrielle Keiller, Ken Powell, and Roland Penrose and his wife Lee Miller, amongst others, which have all been popular with our visitors.

We are particularly grateful to Alan Stewart and his wife Anthea Sieveking, Natalie's youngest daughter from her first marriage, for their wholehearted support of this project. Anthony d'Offay introduced Mr and Mrs Stewart to the National Galleries of Scotland, from which happy meeting has grown this project. We would also like to thank all the lenders to the exhibition. We are indebted to the various contributors to the book: Frances Stenlake for her discussion of Bobby Bevan's promotion of his father's work, Caroline Cuthbert and Dick Chapman for their personal reminiscences, and Kirstie Meehan, Melissa Munro and Lauren Rigby from the Scottish National Gallery of Modern Art for their research. Finally, we would like to thank Alice Strang and her colleagues at the National Galleries of Scotland who have brought their customary enthusiasm to this publication and exhibition, which are dedicated to the memory of Natalie Bevan.

JOHN LEIGHTON
Director-General
National Galleries of Scotland

SIMON GROOM
Director of Modern and Contemporary Art
National Galleries of Scotland

Acknowledgements

THIS publication represents the first time that the art of Boxted has been researched in depth and little has been published about the post-World War Two arts scene in Colchester. The author is, therefore, particularly indebted to the following people for the generous sharing of their expertise: Michael and Lucy Archer, Anthony Atkinson; Evelyne Conrad-Bell of The Victor Batte-Lay Trust; Dr Ronald Blythe; Wendy Baron; Dick Chapman; Caroline Cuthbert; Alan Ellis of Colchester Art Society; Frederick Gore; Maggi Hambling; Sarah MacDougall; Anthony d'Offay; Anthea Sieveking; Frances Stenlake, and Alan Stewart.

The following people have also provided invaluable information: Martyn Anglesea, Ulster Museum; Annette Armstrong; Elaine Blake, Reading Museum Service; Sophie Bowness; Professor Andrew Causey; Peter Collingwood; Anna Cookson; Barry Cox, June Searby and Chloë Veale, The History of Advertising Trust; Janey Cronyn; Robert S. Davey; Dudley Diaper, Colchester Library; Ben Duncan; James Elliott, Anthony d'Offay Ltd; Mary Fedden; Allen Freer; Jane Furness, Edinburgh College of Art; Luke Gertler; Hilary Guest, Underwood & Company; Robert Hall, Huddersfield Art Gallery; Colin Harrison, Ashmolean Museum of Art and Archaeology; Michael Hitchon, National Council for the Conservation of Plants & Gardens; Jonathan Horwich and Pippa Jacomb, Christie's; Jayne Knowles, Colchester Institute; Ian Lowe; Annabel Lucas, Firstsite; Anne Lutyens-Humfrey, Chelmsford Museums; Professor Kenneth McConkey; Gavin McEwan, Turcan Connell; Christopher Martin, University of Portsmouth; Sandra Martin, Manchester Art Gallery; Catharine Morris, *The Times*; Diane Perkins and Linda Theophilus, Gainsborough's House; Henrietta Phipps; Antonia Reeve; Denzil Reeves; Daniel Robbins, Leighton House Museum; Geoffrey Russell, The Institute of Practitioners in Advertising; Michael Russell; John Saumarez Smith, G. Heywood Hill Ltd; Anne Seymour; Penelope Sexton, Royal Albert Memorial Museum & Art Gallery, Exeter; Nicholas Skeaping; Gavin, Patsy and Robert Strang; Maggie Thornton, Redfern Gallery; David Tregunna, IAP Fine Art; Robert Upstone, Tate Britain; Associate Professor Dr Michael J.K. Walsh, Eastern Mediterranean University.

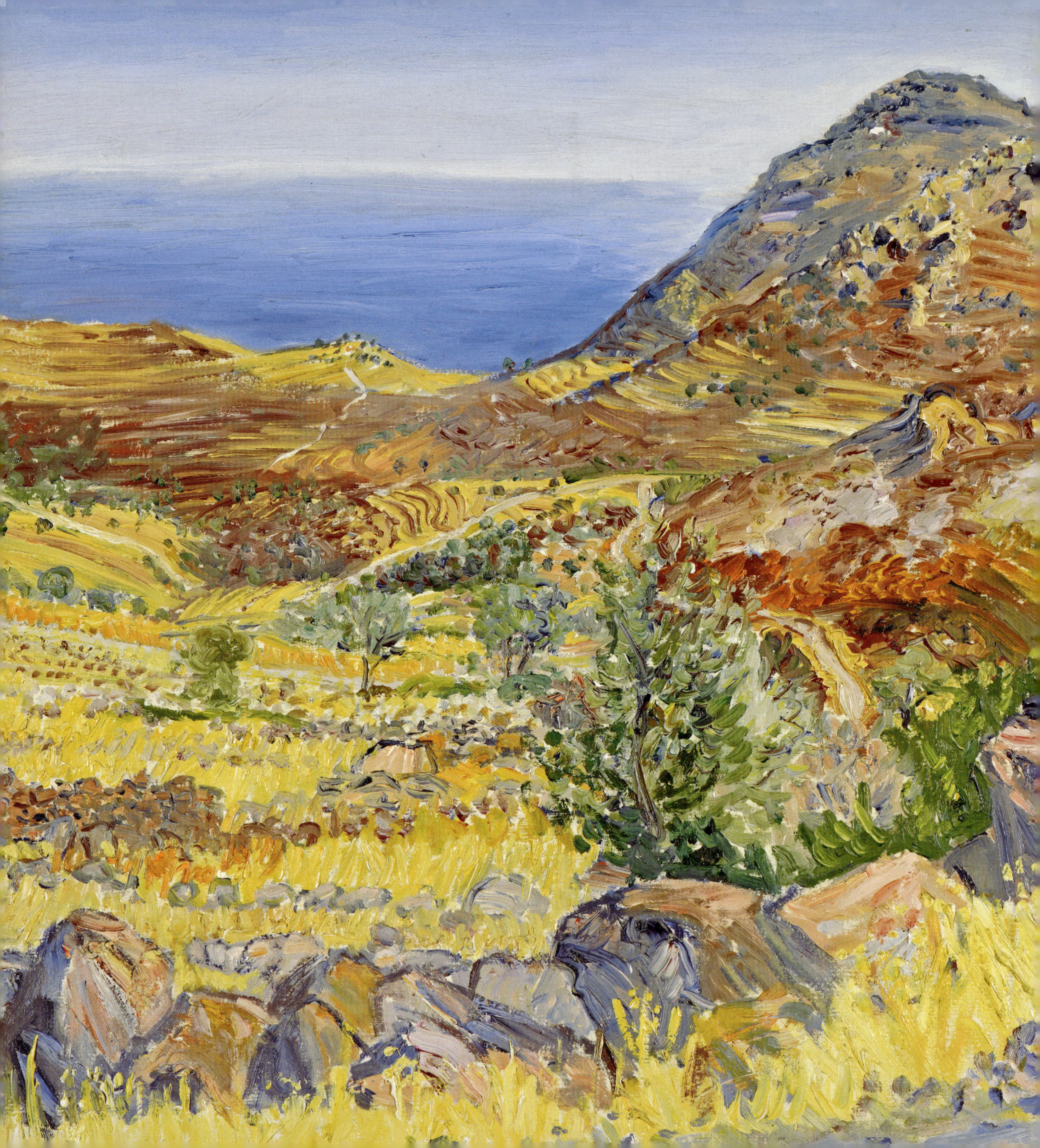

Bobby and Natalie Bevan and the Art at Boxted House

ALICE STRANG

The rooms were crowded with twentieth-century English works … The pictures told of relationships rather than purchases.

RONALD BLYTHE, 2007[1]

BOXTED House, near the Essex-Suffolk border of East Anglia, was the home of Robert Alexander Bevan (Bobby) and his wife Natalie from 1947 until his death in 1974. An extraordinary and very personal art collection hung upon its walls, which reflected three main areas of the Bevans' lives: firstly, work by Bobby's parents, the painters Robert Polhill Bevan and Stanislawa de Karlowska and their friends, including Harold Gilman, Charles Ginner and Walter Sickert; secondly, works by artists such as Mark Gertler, Augustus John and John Armstrong, whom Bobby and Natalie knew independently during the 1920s and 1930s; and finally, works by artists with connections to East Anglia, for example Cedric Morris, Lett Haines and John Nash, who were close friends and neighbours of the couple. A final theme in the collection was Bobby's passion for a catholic range of exceptional works on paper.

Bobby had a distinguished career in the advertising industry, joining the leading London agency S.H. Benson Ltd in 1923. He rose to become chairman in 1954 and stayed in this post until his retirement ten years later.[2] Natalie was a painter and ceramicist. She was encouraged in this field by her mother Alice Denny, who was a children's book illustrator, and by artist friends like Christopher Nevinson and Harry Jonas. In the 1960s she turned her attention to pottery and in 1968 had a solo exhibition at Anthony d'Offay's London gallery.[3]

Bobby and Natalie were generous patrons of the visual arts and as a result they and their house played an important role in the post-war cultural renaissance of East Anglia, centred on Colchester. They had particularly close links with the Minories art gallery, which opened in the town in 1958 and Bobby served as chairman of its management committee, The Victor Batte-Lay Trust, from 1963 until 1974. Natalie attended classes at Colchester School of Art and was an exhibiting member of Colchester Art Society. The couple frequently acquired works from the society's exhibitions, thus providing crucial encouragement to local artists. Bobby, supported by Natalie, also worked tirelessly to promote the work of

Fig. 1 · Frederick Gore, detail from *Looking Towards the Aegean Sea from the Greek Island of Aegina*, 1988
Private collection

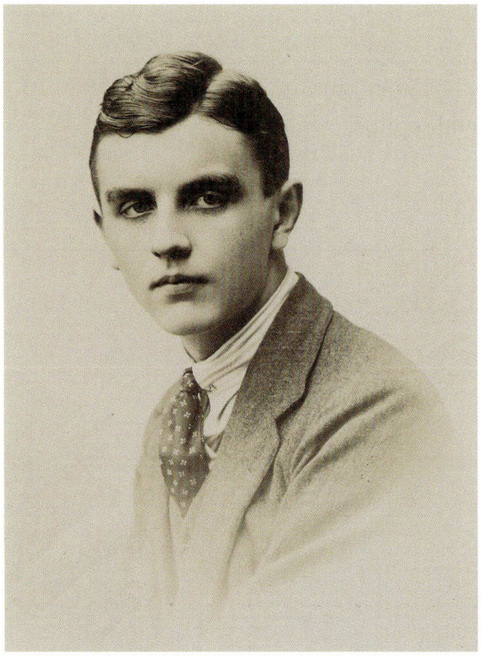

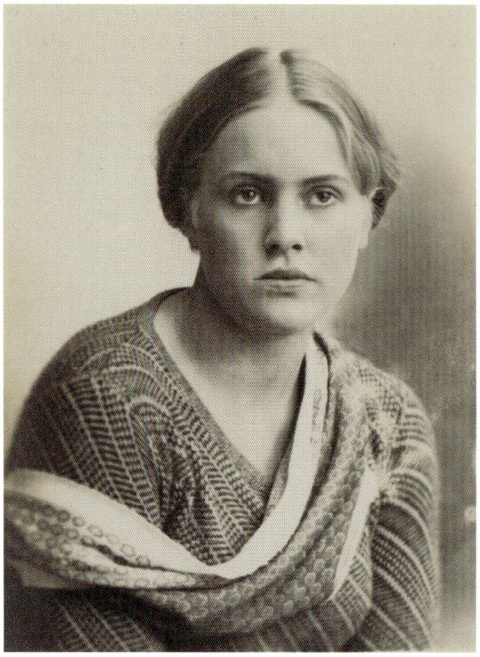

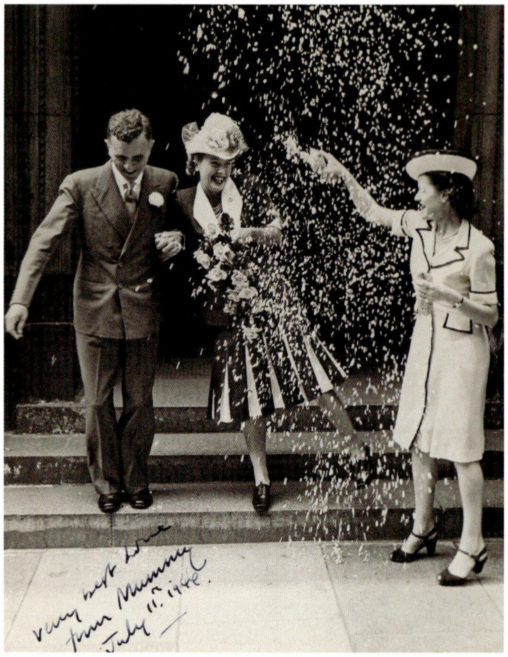

Fig. 2 · Bobby Bevan, *c.*1920
Private collection

Fig. 3 · Natalie Bevan, *c.*1928
Private collection

Fig. 4 · Bobby and Natalie Bevan on their wedding day, 11 July 1946. The photo is inscribed by Natalie to her daughter, Anthea Sieveking.
Private collection

his parents and their contemporaries, as Frances Stenlake discusses in her essay (pp.25–9).

During the 1950s and 1960s, Boxted House became a gathering place not just for artists, but also for writers, politicians, plantsmen-gardeners and other creative individuals. Fine art was just one aspect of the unique environment in which the hospitable Bobby and Natalie lived; friends recall Bobby's collection of eighteenth-century furniture and Natalie's collections of Staffordshire and Chelsea ceramics, amongst other features, which when combined with his wine cellar and her kitchen made each visit an unforgettable experience.

Just to look at your loveliness is a delight to me – a delight of which I never tire ... I think of you always.

BOBBY TO NATALIE, 1928[4]

BOBBY Bevan (1901–1974) and Natalie Denny (1909–2007) met in 1927 [figs.2, 3]. They were part of the avant-garde artistic milieu of London of the late 1920s and many of the friends they made at that time were represented by works at Boxted House. Bobby, a young copywriter for Bensons advertising agency, fell in love with the vivacious fledgling artist Natalie Denny and proposed to her. As the painter Mark Gertler (1891–1939) remarked of Natalie, who modelled for him: 'She is a nice girl, but too popular – there is a waiting list of six men, all of whom have proposed to her – but she cannot as yet make up her mind – meanwhile they all buzz around her like so many amorous bees – what a life!'[5] However, on 24 August 1929, Natalie married another member of their circle, the writer and pioneering radio and television producer Lancelot de Giberne Sieveking (1896–1972).[6] They lived in London and Snape, Suffolk and had two daughters, the painter Victoria Burroughs (1930–1993) and the photographer Anthea Sieveking (b.1933).

Natalie and Lance Sieveking were divorced in 1943. On his return from service as Chief of Naval Information at the British Admiralty in Washington, Bobby was delighted to discover that Natalie was single once more.[7] Some twenty years after Bobby's first proposal, Natalie accepted him and they were married in London on 11 July 1946.

The Bevans' marriage [fig.4] coincided with Bobby's postwar reclamation of Boxted House, which he had bought in 1938. The grey-brick Georgian house of 1820 appealed to his love of classical architecture. However, World War Two broke out before he was able to move in and the house was requisitioned by the Army. Immediately after their wedding, the couple set about decorating and furnishing their country retreat. From 1947 it became their home, although they maintained a flat in Knightsbridge until Bobby's retirement in 1964.

East Anglia, in the south-east of England, consists of the counties of Norfolk, Suffolk and Essex. Dependent almost entirely on agriculture, it was a quiet, remote, unfashionable area with good, affordable housing, as well as distinguished architecture, and an efficient train service from Colchester, which made commuting to London possible. It had a significant creative heritage as its rural life, vast skies, characteristic flatlands and waterways and quality of light have attracted artists since the eighteenth century. This provided inspiration for its leading native masters, Thomas Gainsborough (1727–1788), John Crome (1768–1821) and John Constable (1776–1837) and gave rise to the renowned nineteenth-century Norwich School of artists.

Natalie was already intimate with the area having lived in Suffolk during the 1930s with her first husband. Moreover, during World War Two, she organised the collection of scrap metal throughout the region for the Ministry of Works. The Sievekings and Bobby were amongst many people, particularly those of an artistic bent, who were attracted to East Anglia in the mid-twentieth century.

Boxted House was situated in a large garden which included a walled kitchen garden, a terrace, arbour and pond, as well as a lake. The house consisted of three principal rooms on the ground floor; the drawing-room, with a view across the croquet lawn to the meadows beyond; the library, which Bobby used as his study; and the dining-room, with French windows which opened on to the terrace. Natalie's sitting-room was on the other side of the hall and gave on to a large conservatory-studio, containing her kiln and easels. A passageway led past a cloakroom and butler's pantry to the kitchen. Stairs from the hall led to seven bedrooms, one

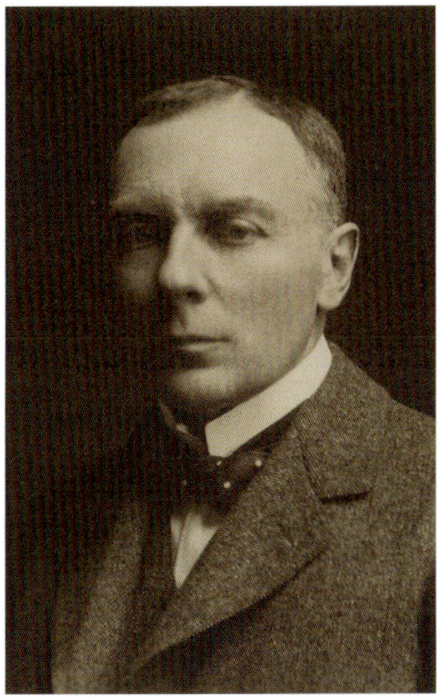

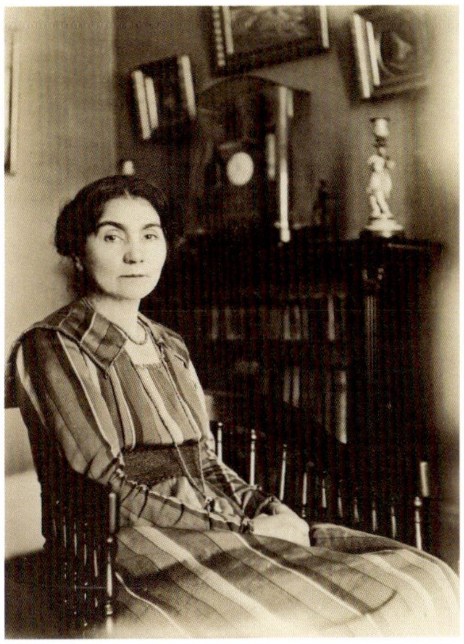

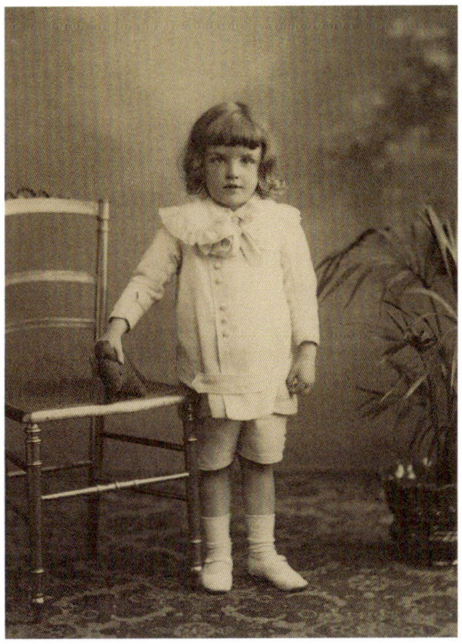

Fig. 5 · Robert Bevan, *c.*1910
Private collection

Fig. 6 · Stanislawa de Karlowska, *c.*1910
Private collection

Fig. 7 · Bobby Bevan, *c.*1905
Private collection

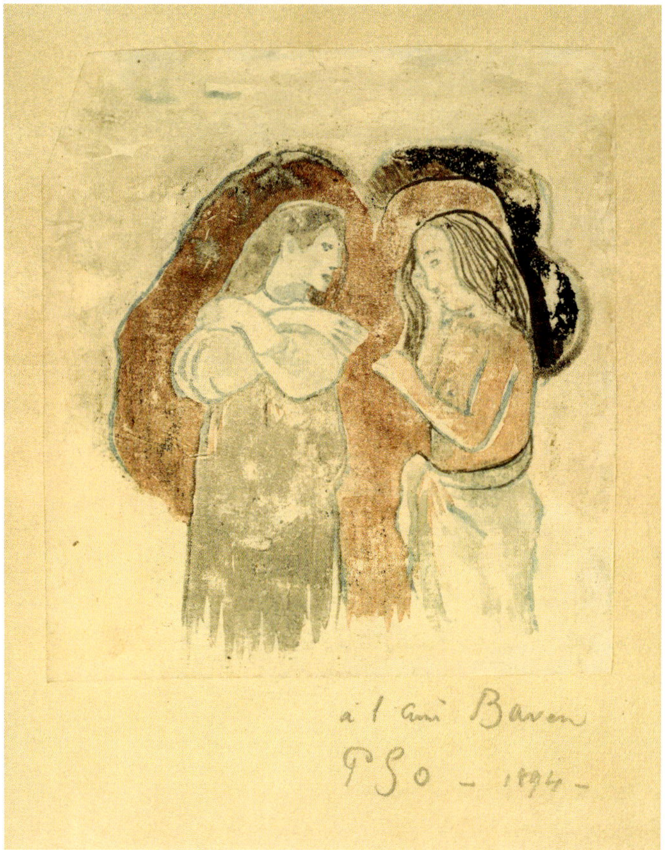

Fig. 8 · Paul Gauguin
Two Tahitian Girls, 1894
Private collection

of which was given over to the storage of works and was known as the picture room. Three bathrooms completed the accommodation. For almost thirty years, the Bevans hung their ever-growing and changing collection of art on these walls.

I have known most of the artists, some of them extremely well. Gore, Gilman and Ginner were the most intimate with my father, and all my life I have considered their work to be of great moment in the history of English twentieth-century art.

BOBBY BEVAN, 1969[8]

AT the heart of the collection at Boxted House was an impressive group of works by Bobby's parents, Robert Polhill Bevan (1865–1925) and Stanislawa de Karlowska (1876–1952) and their friends and contemporaries [figs.5, 6]. They included Harold Gilman (1876–1919), Charles Ginner (1878–1952), Spencer Gore (1878–1914) and Walter Sickert (1860–1942), who were closely associated with each other during the 1910s. Most were members of the London-based independent exhibiting groups which showcased their Post-Impressionist art and which played a considerable role in the development of modern British art, namely the Fitzroy Street Group, founded in 1907; the Allied Artists Association, founded in 1908; the Camden Town Group, founded in 1911; the London Group, founded in 1913 and the Cumberland Market Group, founded in 1914.

Robert Bevan was born in Hove, East Sussex in 1865. He attended Westminster School of Art and the Académie Julian in Paris. In 1890–1 and 1893–4 he worked in Pont-Aven, Brittany and met Paul Gauguin (1848–1903), a pioneer of the Post-Impressionist movement, who had a significant influence on Bevan and many other artists of his generation. Bobby and Natalie were particularly proud of a monotype which Gauguin made and gave to Bevan during the summer of 1894 and which he dedicated 'à l'ami Baven [*sic*]' [fig.8].

In 1897, Bevan met the artist Stanislawa de Karlowska at the wedding of his friend Eric Forbes-Robertson. Born in 1876 to land-owning gentry in Russian-occupied Poland, Karlowska had also studied at the Académie Julian, though in 1896, seven years after Bevan. They married in 1897 and in 1900 the couple moved to 14 Adamson Road, Swiss Cottage, London, which remained their home for the rest of Bevan's lifetime.

Bevan and Karlowska were central figures in the London art scene before and after World War One. Their careers and professional connections, and also Bobby's childhood, could be surveyed throughout Boxted House. Bevan's impressionist painting *The Gate at Szeliwy*, 1901 [plate 7] hung in Natalie's sitting-room, and shows Karlowska with Bobby's sister Edith (1898–1984), who was also known as Halszka, outside their maternal family's estate in Poland. Bevan's extraordinarily advanced *Study for 'The Courtyard'*, *c.*1904 [plate 8], with its Fauvist palette, was displayed on an easel in the picture room. The tranquil evocation of the beauty of the English countryside around Bevan's own childhood home in West Sussex, *Gravelye Farm, Cuckfield*, *c.*1911 [plate 10], hung in the drawing-room, which was dominated by his magnificent *Showing at Tattersall's*, 1919 [plate 14]. This is a fine example of the celebrated images of London horse sales with which, alongside his paintings of horse-cab yards, Bevan made his name. Bobby often accompanied his father on sketching trips to these increasingly outmoded locations. In 1957 Bobby gave *Showing at Tattersall's* to the Ashmolean Museum, Oxford, as part of a significant gift of works by his father and other Camden Town Group painters; he also gave a purchase fund with which to acquire further related works for its collection.[9] A representative range of Bevan's particularly fine lithographs and other works on paper, including the last drawing he ever made, *The Cottage on the Common* of 1925, could be seen in more intimate corners of Boxted House.

Stanislawa de Karlowska's achievements were often overshadowed by those of her husband, but she was a founding member of the London Group and exhibited regularly with them for more than thirty years, as well as in other significant group exhibitions, such as those of the New English Art Club, Goupil Gallery Salon and the Society of Wood Engravers. Her favoured subjects were London squares and houses, and West Country scenes, as seen in *Backs of Houses, Percy Street*, *c.*1919 and *The Stable Field, Horsgate*, *c.*1914 [plate 28, 27]. A good range of Karlowska's work was always on view in her son's home.

Bevan and Karlowska themselves collected major works by their contemporaries and many of the works remained with their family, while Bobby and Natalie acquired related paintings of the same calibre as they came on to the art market. For example, Bevan swapped his *The Town Field, Horsgate*, 1914, now in the collection of Reading Museum Service, with Charles Ginner, for the latter's *La Vieille Balayeuse, Dieppe*, 1913 [plate 24], while Bobby purchased Sickert's depiction of a desperate game of baccarat being played in the casino at Dieppe, *The System*, 1924–8 [plate 35], from The Mayor Gallery, London in 1951.[10] Sickert was a father-figure to most of the groups with which Bevan and Karlowska were associated and on introducing Bobby [fig. 7] to the great man, Bevan said: 'Sickert, I want my son to meet you. He has heard a lot about you.'[11]

Indeed, Bobby was able to meet and become familiar with many of the leading artists of his parents' generation at their popular Sunday 'at homes'. The paintings at Boxted House revealed the intimate friendships between their creators. Thus Harold Gilman's sensitive, unfinished portrait of Spencer Gore of about 1911–12 [plate 20], hung in the dining-room.[12] Gilman and Gore met whilst studying at the Slade School of Fine Art in London in the 1890s. Together, they saw Bevan's work for the first time at the Allied Artists Association exhibition of 1908. As a result, they invited him to join Sickert's Fitzroy Street Group and Bevan was ushered into the heart of a loose association of pioneering artists. Gilman went on to paint three portraits of Karlowska, including *Mrs Robert Bevan*, of about 1913 [plate 22], which Bobby purchased in 1964, whilst his sensual *Nude at a Window*, of about 1912 [plate 23] was hung in the library, visible only to those invited into Bobby's private study.[13]

Amongst the works which Bobby and

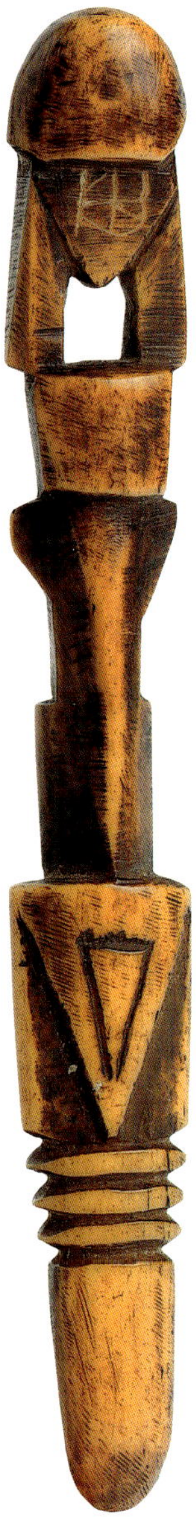

Fig. 9 · Henri Gaudier-Brzeska, *Ornament*, 1914
Anthony d'Offay, London

Fig. 10 · Henri Gaudier-Brzeska, *Horse*, 1913
Private collection

Natalie especially treasured, were sculptures and drawings by the French artist Henri Gaudier-Brzeska (1891–1915). He and his partner, the Polish writer Sophie Brzeska (1871–1925), whose surname he added to his own and to whom he referred to as his sister because of their unmarried status, became very close to Bevan and Karlowska in the early 1910s. The vital practical support Bobby's parents gave to the poverty-stricken couple is exemplified by Karlowska's purchase, for ten shillings, of Gaudier's *Ornament* of 1914 [fig.9], which he carved from a bone-handled toothbrush as he was unable to afford proper materials.[14] After Gaudier enlisted as a soldier in World War One, Karlowska regularly sent him supplies of comforts such as cigarettes and chocolate. Perhaps the greatest testimony to their closeness was the letter Gaudier wrote to her from the trenches on 1 January 1915, saying: 'Since I might fall, would you be so kind as to ask for my news from Capt. Ménager … to send to my sister.'[15]

Gaudier was killed in action five months later and Bevan helped organise a memorial exhibition of his work at the Leicester Galleries, London in 1918.

The Cave of Harmony, the Gargoyle, endless lovely parties and beautiful, beautiful people; but most of all the long serious talks about Painting and Love made a golden glorious beginning to our life-long friendship.

NATALIE ON JOHN ARMSTRONG, 1977[16]

THE contents of Boxted House also bore witness to the friendships Bobby and Natalie formed with artists of their own age in the heady days of London during the late 1920s. Like Bobby, Natalie grew up in London, in Kensington. On 'coming out' into society (although not in the official sense) in 1927 and as an extremely beautiful and charismatic eighteen-year old, she soon became popular within the artistic milieu centred on nightclubs such as The Cave of Harmony and The Gargoyle and studio-parties hosted by the likes of Augustus John and frequented by former Slade students. Bobby, by his birthright, was already a member of this extraordinary community.

It was at a New Year's Eve party held by John in 1927 that Natalie met Mark Gertler. He was so taken with her that just two weeks later he wrote: 'I wonder if you are free on Sunday afternoon, if so would you come over and let me see you in my Studio … I shouldn't do much more than just find the pose on the first occasion.'[17] As a result, Natalie sat for two portraits by Gertler, the most magnificent of which, *Supper (Natalie Denny)* of 1928 [plate 19] Bobby was able to buy for her after their marriage. It hung in pride of place at Boxted House, above the fireplace in the drawing-room.

Bobby was one of a new breed of university-educated, young creative types then beginning to transform the world of advertising by introducing the embryonic concepts of consumer psychology, market research, strategic planning and branding. Not long after graduating from

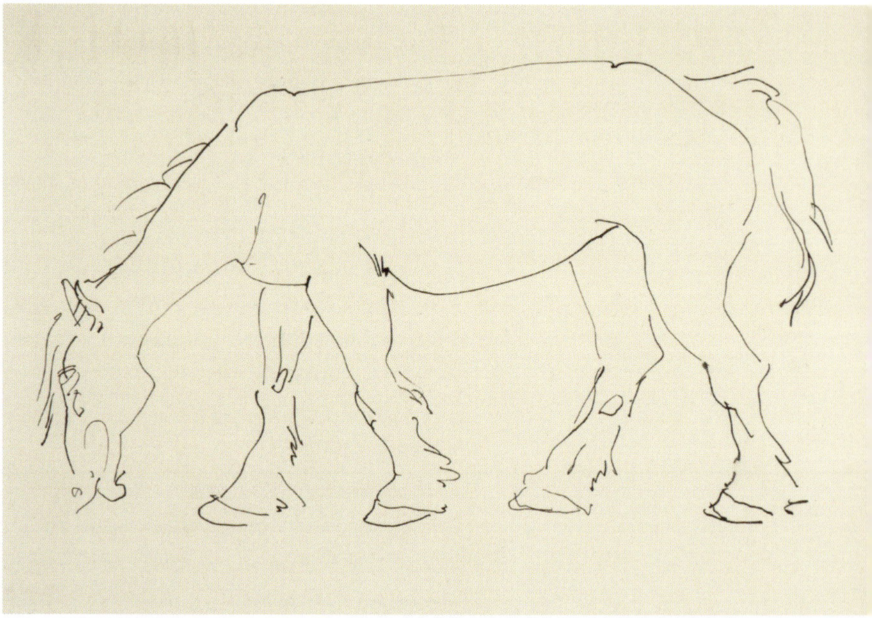

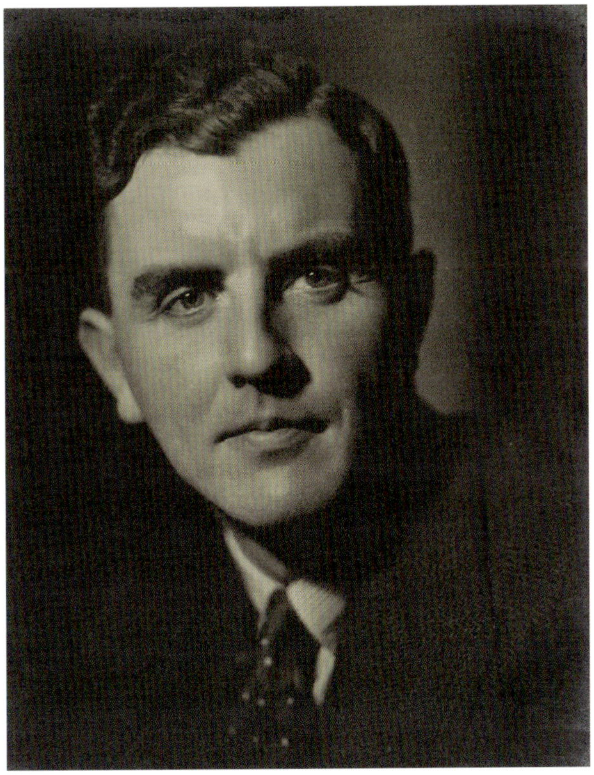

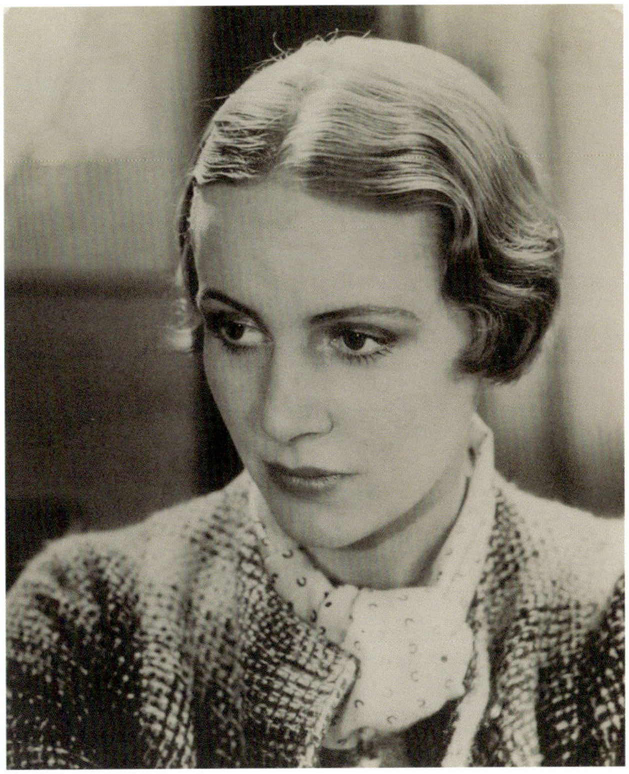

Fig. 11 · Bobby Bevan, *c.*1945
Private collection

Fig. 12 · Natalie Bevan in the mid-1930s.
Private collection

Christ Church, Oxford, he joined Bensons' 'Literary Department' as a copywriter. When Guinness decided to advertise for the first time in 1928, they approached Bensons and Bobby began a long association with the famous campaigns under the still familiar slogan 'Guinness is Good For You'. His colleague Dorothy L. Sayers immortalised Bobby, at this stage in his life, as the affable Mr Ingleby in her popular murder mystery of 1933, *Murder Must Advertise*, which was set in a barely-disguised Bensons.[18]

Another writer amongst Natalie and Bobby's crowd was Anthony Powell (1905–2000), who was to visit them in East Anglia. He summed up the eclecticism of the people with whom they mixed in his autobiography, recalling:

Most of those present at a 'typical' party would be likely to possess some connection with the arts ... but never enough of any one calling to make the assembly a painters' party, an actors' party, an ad-men's party, though several painters would be likely to be present, the stray actor and ad-man ... There would be occasional musicians; architects; photographers ... The girls, largely drawn from the all-inclusive ... vocation of model ... usually showed an altogether exceptional standard of looks.[19]

Amongst the people that Natalie met in this way and who were to become particularly close friends, was the painter John Armstrong (1893–1973). In 1927 Armstrong was on the cusp of making a name for himself and his first solo exhibition, held at the Leicester Galleries, London the following year, was a great success. The beginning of Natalie and Armstrong's friendship was represented at Boxted House by his *Velocitor* of 1930–1 [plate 1], which reveals his early experimentation with Surrealism. The longevity of their relationship could be seen in Armstrong's *Still Life with Leeks* [plate 2] which he painted whilst staying with the Bevans in Boxted House during the winter of 1955.[20]

Bobby, Natalie and Armstrong had

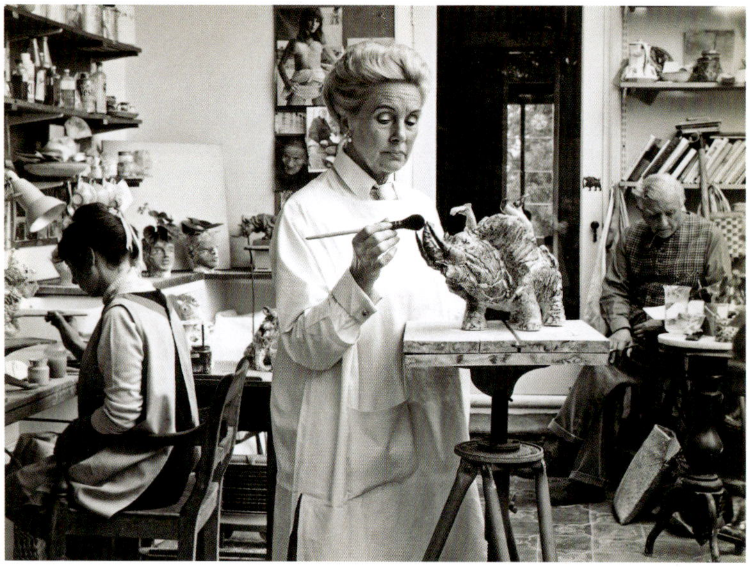

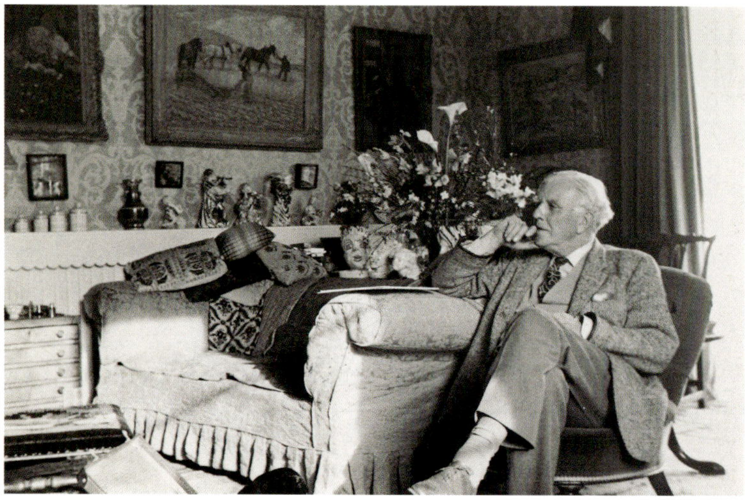

Fig. 13 · Natalie Bevan working in her studio in the conservatory at Boxted House with Audrey Durnan, her glazing assistant, to the left and Bobby Bevan on the right, *c.*1968.
Private collection

Fig. 14 · Bobby Bevan in the drawing-room at Boxted House in 1968. Paintings by Sickert, Bevan, Gilman and Natalie Bevan are visible on the walls [plates 22, 35].
Private collection

many friends in common, including Lance Sieveking and the artists Harry Jonas (1893–1990) and C.R.W. Nevinson (1889–1946). In 1967, Natalie recalled how in 1928 'on a golden summer's day I put on a huge purple hat … packed a little bag mostly full of water-colour paints … and set off with Harry Jonas, Richard Nevinson and his wife Kathleen on a painting holiday.'[21] That Natalie was allowed, aged eighteen, to travel to Paris unchaperoned in this way, speaks volumes for the liberalism of her parents. As Natalie had little money of her own at this point, it is likely that Bobby bought Nevinson's *Broadway Girls* and *The Lilies of the Café*, both of about 1919 [plates 33, 34] for her after World War Two.[22] Their family thought the former summed up Natalie's own joie de vivre.

Naturally, there were some artists who knew Robert Bevan and Stanislawa de Karlowska, who died in 1925 and 1952 respectively, and who were also part of Bobby and Natalie's circle. For example, Nevinson and Gertler were members of the London Group, while John Nash (1893–1977) had been a young member of the Camden Town Group, London Group and Cumberland Market Group with Bevan. As Nash first exhibited with his father in 1913, Bobby would have known him from the age of twelve. Nash was the younger brother of the painter Paul Nash (1889–1946), who met Lance Sieveking in the Artists' Rifles in 1914. Both Nash brothers illustrated books by Natalie's first husband and John Nash was to become one of her most long-standing friends.[23] Frederick Gore (b.1913), the artist son of Bevan's close ally Spencer Gore, was a friend of Bobby's from childhood. Natalie became very fond of him and as a result, she hung Freddie's *Looking Towards the Aegean Sea from the Greek Island of Aegina* of 1988 [fig.1], above the sofa in her sitting-room, just across the hall from his father's beautifully modest *Conversation Piece and Self-portrait* of *c.*1910 [plate 25], which could be seen in the library.

It was an utter pleasure to go for a walk with John – everything came to life and looked more interesting through his eyes. Even fishing was a pleasure; sitting beside him and listening to him talking about the landscape and the sky, and all the different lights and shades and shadows.

NATALIE ON JOHN NASH, 1983[24]

THE art at Boxted House was not only by artists of their parents' generation and by friends made before their marriage, but also bore witness to Bobby and Natalie's whole-hearted involvement with the flourishing arts scene centred on Colchester after World War Two. They and their Essex-Suffolk associates were stalwarts of the Minories, which opened in 1958, Colchester Art Society, founded in 1946, Colchester School of Art and the East Anglian School of Painting and Drawing in Hadleigh, run by the Bevans' friends Cedric Morris and Lett Haines.

Amongst the many artists drawn to East Anglia at this time were John Nash and his wife Christine Kühlenthal (1895–1976). Two years before Bobby and Natalie moved to Boxted House, the Nashes had settled six miles away at Bottengoms Farm, Wormingford. Also nearby were the painters and partners Cedric Morris (1889–1982) and Lett Haines (1894–1978), whose home and acclaimed art school were based at Benton End. Bobby and Natalie had met both couples in London before the war, but the relationship between the neighbours blossomed in the late 1940s and they formed the core of the Boxted House social circle.

John Nash found infinite inspiration in his garden at Bottengoms and the countryside around the Stour Valley in which he lived, despite Sickert describing it as having been left 'a sucked orange' by Gainsborough and Constable.[25] This can be seen in his tender *Ice and Snow*, 1959 [plate 32], which depicts the ponds at Bottengoms in winter and which Bobby purchased from Nash's 1960 solo exhibition at the Leicester Galleries.

Nash also made many works in the grounds of Boxted House and its vicinity. Several were shown in his vast retrospective exhibition at the Royal Academy of Arts, London, in 1967, to which the Bevans were generous lenders, and which included *The Lake at Boxted House* of 1962, now in the collection of Chelmsford and Essex Museum.[26] Bobby encouraged Nash to raise his modest prices after the success of the exhibition, but to little avail.

Natalie hung many sensitive botanical drawings by Nash in her bedroom at Boxted House, alongside the humorously-illustrated letters which he wrote to her when on holiday, such as *Girls being Tiresome*, 1965 [fig.15]. These comic drawings prompted Bobby to commission Nash, on Guinness's behalf, to illustrate *Happy New Lear*. This was one of the twenty-five Christmas booklets produced by Guinness between 1933 and 1966 to send to medical doctors, presumably to help spread the notion that 'Guinness is Good for You'. *Happy New Lear* contained poems by

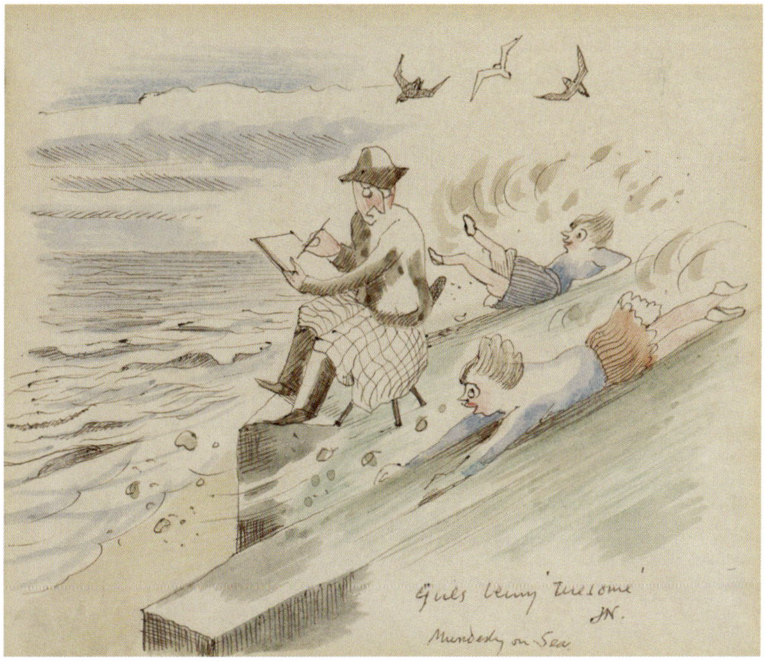

Fig. 15 · John Nash
Girls being Tiresome, 1965
Private collection

Stanley Penn parodying Edward Lear, to whom Nash's aunt had been engaged. It was published in 1957 by W.S. Cowell Ltd of nearby Ipswich. Cowells was a pioneer of lithographic colour printing at this time and employed many East Anglian artists to undertake design, calligraphic and illustrative work.

Bobby and Natalie had met Cedric Morris and Lett Haines in London in the second half of the 1920s. Morris was enjoying a period of great professional success with acclaimed exhibitions at Arthur Tooth & Sons in 1928 and 1930, amongst others. However, he became disillusioned with the commercial art world and in 1929 he and Haines took on the lease of Pound Farm, outside Higham in Suffolk, basing themselves there from 1930. Bobby became an intimate of the Pound community and it was probably at this time that he acquired Morris's forthright *Paysage du Jardin no. 2*, 1931, which hung in the drawing-room at Boxted House, and *The Blue Poppy*, 1932 [plates 29, 30].[27] Both depict flowers which Morris grew at The Pound. Indeed, he and John Nash were so passionate about their gardens that they are more properly described as artist–plantsmen and this shared interest added to the depth of their friendship.

In 1937 Morris and Haines opened their remarkable art school in nearby Dedham: its pupils included Lucian Freud (b. 1922) and later Maggi Hambling (b. 1945), but it was destroyed by fire two years later. This prompted the move to Benton End in 1940, which became known throughout East Anglia, with some suspicion, as 'The Artists' Place'. Morris was to become an iris breeder of international distinction in the 1940s and the garden at Benton End became a place of pilgrimage for horticulturalists.[28]

Fig. 16 · Richard Bedford, *Wood Louse*, 1950s
Private collection

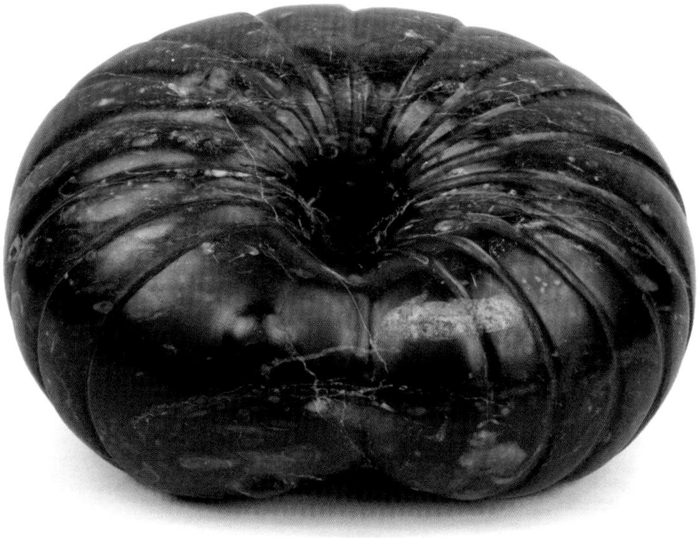

Besides acquiring works for themselves, Bobby and Natalie did what they could to promote Morris's career at large. Thus Bobby purchased his allegorical *Crisis*, 1939 and its partner painting *Yalta*, 1945, with which the artist marked the beginning and end of World War Two, for the collection he established at Bensons.[29] The fact that Morris's 1968 retrospective exhibition toured to the Minories after its inaugural showing at the National Museum of Wales in Cardiff, was in no small part due to Bobby's chairmanship of the Colchester gallery.[30]

Indeed, the art at Boxted House is inextricably entwined with the exhibition programme overseen by Bobby and the Minories' curators Jack Wood Palmer and Michael Chase (1915–2001), which made the gallery one of Britain's leading art centres in the 1960s. Artists granted solo shows included figureheads of the Bevans' collection, such as Robert Bevan (1965), Mark Gertler (1971) and Harold Gilman (1969), as well as contemporaries like John Nash (1967) and Cedric Morris (1968).

Bobby and Natalie's collection also contained works by leading lights of Colchester Art Society, many acquired at the society's annual exhibitions held at the Minories from its opening in 1958 until its closure in 1992. Founded in 1946 by Reg Hazell, then Head of Colchester School of Art, Morris, Nash and others, the society operated an 'open' policy of showing work selected purely on merit, whether its creator was a professional or amateur artist. The Bevans' acquisitions provided vital encouragement to their local creators, who were often welcomed to Boxted House. Works by artists including John Addyman (1929–2006), Anthony Atkinson (b. 1929) - who was Head of Colchester School of Art from 1964 until 1975, Richard Bedford (1883–1967) – whose tactile work titled *Wood Louse* [fig. 16] was one of the few sculptures that Bobby purchased – Peter

Coker (1926–2004), Denzil Reeves (b. 1926) – from whom the Bevans commissioned a woodcut of their house [half-title] – and the Aldeburgh-based Mary Potter (1900–1981), encompassed the development of the visual arts in the area in the 1950s and 1960s.

Boxted House also contained numerous paintings and ceramics by Natalie herself. After her unorthodox training by artist-friends in 1920s London, Natalie's art flourished during her first marriage. Throughout the 1930s, she concentrated on painting in oils and watercolours, creating lively images of the Suffolk landscape, as well as of France and Mexico. Following her marriage to Bobby, Natalie became immersed in supporting his burgeoning career, but by 1958 she was a member and exhibitor with Colchester Art Society, remaining involved with their activities for over thirty years; in the 1960s she exhibited every year with the society and served twice on its general committee.[31]

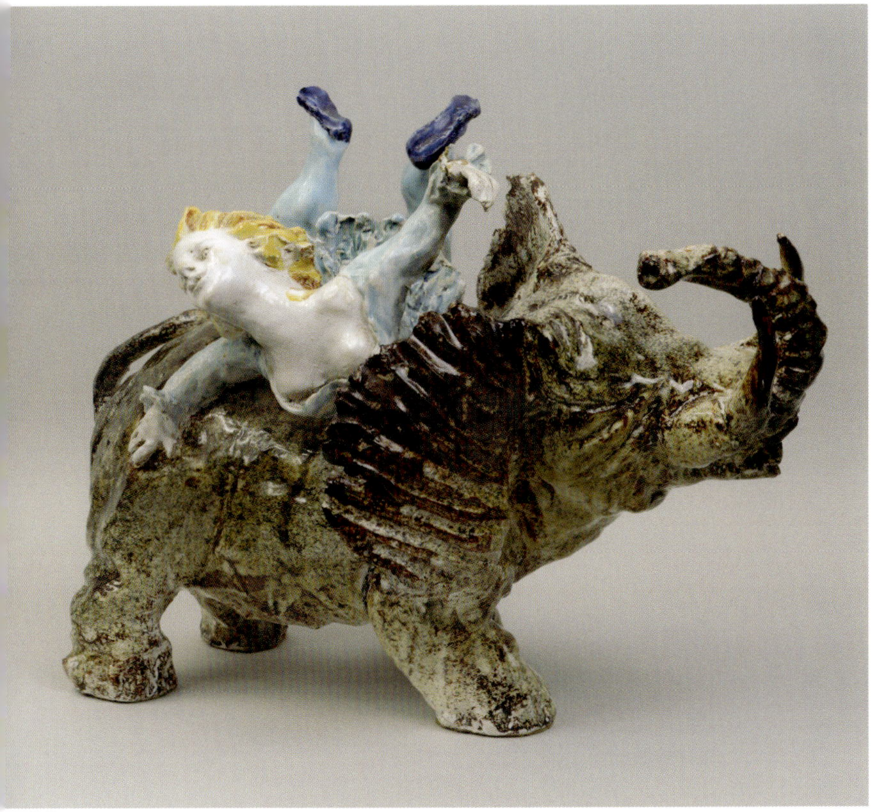

It was at this time that Natalie wholeheartedly resumed her own artistic activities, attending classes at Colchester School of Art, founded in 1885, which maintained a benevolent, if distant, relationship with its bohemian neighbour, the East Anglian School of Painting and Drawing. Many of the staff at the School of Art had trained at the Royal College of Art in London and some also taught there part-time, not least John Nash, helping to make this one of the most creative periods in the school's history.[32]

However, in the early 1960s Natalie became interested in the creative potential of the mud in the lake at Boxted House and turned her attention to the field of ceramics. She attended classes at Chelsea Pottery in London and in 1963 a new conservatory-studio was added to Boxted, housing Natalie's kiln and easels amidst a profusion of greenery. She soon became accomplished at modelling clay, making domestically-scaled circus figures and animals infused with her inimitable energy and sense of fun, such as *Elephant and Columbine* [fig. 17]. Natalie's artistic career climaxed in a solo exhibition of her ceramics at Anthony d'Offay's gallery in London in 1968.

Fig. 17 · Natalie Bevan, *Elephant and Columbine*, *c.*1968
Private collection

Since he had a true collector's eye he did not just buy names; he only acquired works which represented the artists at their highest standards.

GRAHAM REYNOLDS ON BOBBY, 1978[33]

A FURTHER theme within the art on display at Boxted House was Bobby's wide-ranging enthusiasm for outstanding works on paper. As a result, his dressing-room and the landings and passages (where light levels were low enough not to cause damage) were hung with works of particular beauty and skill, such as Paul Cézanne's *Portrait of Guillaumin with Hanged Man* of 1873, Francisco de

Goya's *The Agility and Audacity of Juanito Apinani in the Ring at Madrid* from *La Tauromaquia* of 1816 [fig. 18] and several prints by the seventeenth-century master-etcher Wenceslaus Hollar (1607–1677). Given his own profession, it is not surprising that Bobby also collected examples of the promotional work of artists such as Henri de Toulouse-Lautrec (1864–1901) and Théophile-Alexandre Steinlen (1859–1923), whilst an impressive array of watercolours by Thomas Rowlandson (1756–1827) hinted at his sense of humour.

As could be seen throughout Boxted House, this very personal area in the collection also reflected Bobby's links with East Anglia and his own friendships with artists who had been close to his parents. Thus, drawings by George Clausen (1852–1944), who worked in Essex in the 1890s and during the inter-war period, could be seen alongside woodcuts by Edward O'Rorke Dickey, including *Embankment Jive* of the 1920s. Dickey often attended Robert Bevan and Stanislawa de Karlowska's 'at homes' and showed alongside them in London Group exhibitions from 1920. He became close to Bobby in his own right during his time as the first curator of the Minories from 1957 until 1962.

All of us, painting or writing, felt at home with these Bevan interiors … The atmosphere was laced, as it were, with famous art connections but was at the same time warm and casual.

RONALD BLYTHE, 2007[34]

DURING the 1950s and 1960s, Boxted House became a gathering place for a wide range of visitors, not only for artists; Bobby and Natalie's art collection was just one aspect of the stimulating environment which they created in their home. The Bevans maintained a virtual 'open house' and weekend parties would often include artists such as Edward Ardizzone (1900–1979), whom Bobby commissioned to work for Bensons, Michael Ayrton (1921–1975), Edward Bawden (1903–1989), Dicky Chopping (b.1917) and Denis Wirth-Miller (b.1915) – who had a house in Wivenhoe and who once brought Francis Bacon with them – Maggi Hambling, John Lewis (1912–1996), who acted as typographic consultant for Bensons and shared Bobby's passion for sailing, Morris, Haines and the Nashes.[35] As Hambling recently recalled of her first visit, aged sixteen:

The atmosphere was sophisticated, rather laissez-faire, even decadent, or so it appeared to me at that age. I remember the people and the gin more than the pictures, but there were several Letts and the Bevans had marvellous paintings by Cedric … Natalie's charisma, flowers everywhere and laughter over lavish dinners … I would describe the whole effect as voluptuous.[36]

Bobby and Natalie's social circle also included plantsmen–gardeners, such as Great Bardfield-based John Aldridge (1905–1983) and Richard Bedford, themselves as much artist–plantsmen as Morris and Nash. Nash illustrated several

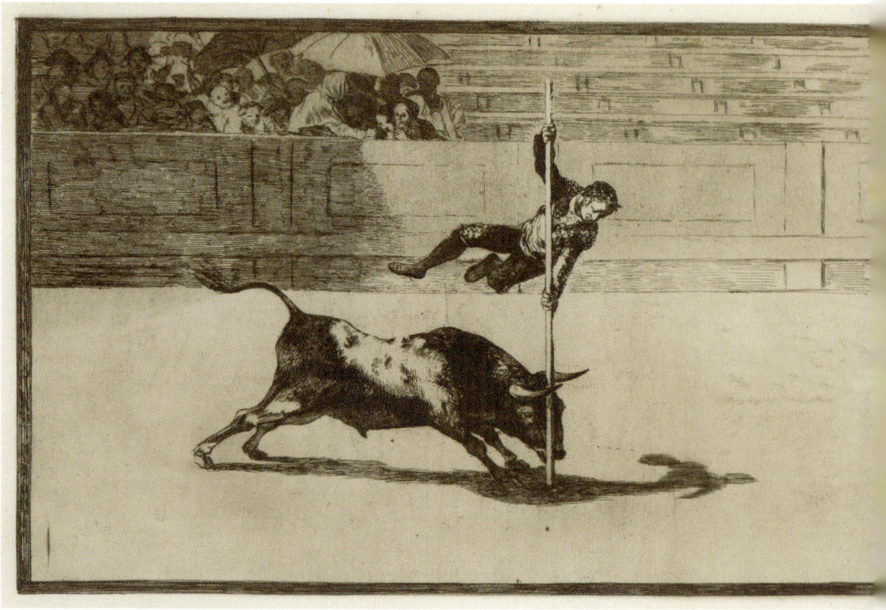

Fig. 18 · Francisco de Goya
'*The Agility and Audacity of Juanito Apinani in the Ring at Madrid*', plate 20 of *La Tauromaquia*, 1816
Private collection

gardening books by Robert Gathorne-Hardy (1902–1973) who visited from time to time, as did Beth Chatto (b.1923). In 1960, Chatto began work on her now celebrated gardens in Elmstead Market, near Colchester, partly inspired by Morris and his garden. The Dedham-based classical architect Raymond Erith (1904–1973) and his wife Pamela (1910–1987) were friends with Bobby in particular, who had at one stage considered a career in architecture, whilst Madge Garland (1898–1990), Professor of Fashion at the Royal College of Art, was close to Natalie.[37]

Visiting writers included Ronald Blythe (b.1922), who has chronicled much of the life of East Anglia during this period, not least in his 1969 novel *Akenfield*, based on the village of Charsfield, Suffolk, and who was particularly close to John and Christine Nash. Anthony Powell was a friend from 1920s London, who made his name with the twelve volume novel *A Dance to the Music of Time*.[38] Powell's *Punch* colleague, the author and politician A.P. Herbert (1890–1971), also knew the Bevans from before their marriage and it was at a summer party at his Chiswick Mall house in 1928 that Natalie was introduced to Lance Sieveking.[39] The humorist Paul Jennings (1918–1989) and author John Leslie (1885–1971) were other key figures in the literary set at Boxted House, reflecting Bobby's fervent interest in literature.

Leading figures in the East Anglian and London art worlds, such as the Minories curator Michael Chase and his wife, the artist Valerie Thornton (1931–1991), and the gallerist Anthony d'Offay (b.1940) and his wife, the art historian Anne Seymour (b.1941) – who once brought the artists Gilbert & George with them to Boxted House – were regular guests. Bobby and Natalie worked closely with Anthony d'Offay on a series of exhibitions of the work of Robert Bevan and other Camden Town Group painters during the 1960s and 1970s, doing much to bring their achievements back into the public

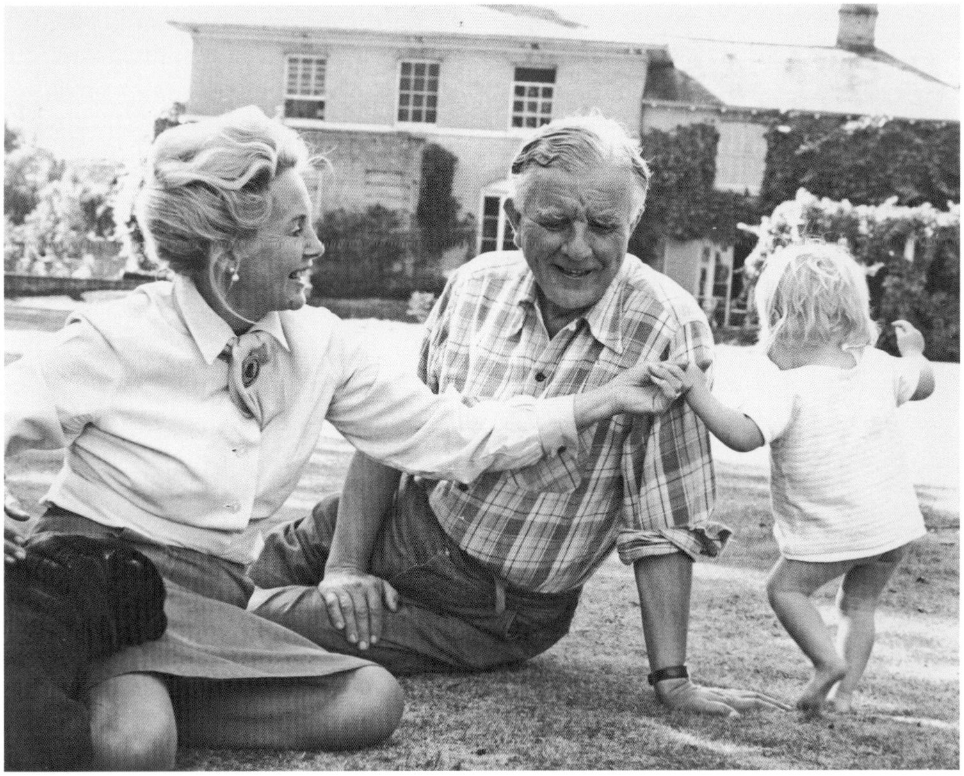

Fig. 19 · Natalie and Bobby Bevan on the lawn at Boxted House, with their granddaughter, Harriet Stewart, in 1964.
Private collection

eye.[40] Shortly after Bobby's death in 1974, Anthony d'Offay recalled his introduction to Boxted House:

I shall never forget that first visit: the house filled with sunlight, paintings, books, flowers and comfortable chairs. Long windows opened on to terraces leading to the garden with croquet lawn, apple orchards and a lake beyond. It was the most welcoming house imaginable. The paintings and books were mostly Bobby's, everything else was due to his wife Natalie, who was not only extraordinarily beautiful but a gifted artist, diarist, cook, gardener and party giver.[41]

Local notables such as the fourth Earl of Cranbrook, Jock Gathorne-Hardy (1900–1978) and his wife, Fidelity Seebohm, the Countess of Cranbrook (b.1912) would call round, sometimes with their co-founders in 1948 of the Aldeburgh Festival, the composer Benjamin Britten (1913–1976) and the tenor Peter Pears (1910–1986). Through the Minories, the Bevans also knew their fellow local collectors of modern art, Marian Benham (1911–1984), of Nayland in Suffolk, who was close friends with Cedric Morris, and the farmer Frank Girling (1898–1966) of Lawford in Essex, who had a particular interest in the Camden Town painters.

Bobby was something of a mentor to the New York-based advertising executive David Ogilvy (1911–1999), who would stay whilst on trips to England. In 1948, with Ogilvy's brother Francis, Bobby had established David as the head of a new agency in New York, aware of the need to break into the American market. The agency, known as Ogilvy, Benson and Mather from 1952, was tremendously successful; in 1964 it merged with Francis's agency, Mather and Crowther to become Ogilvy and Mather International Inc, which in turn acquired S.H. Benson Ltd in 1971, seven years after Bobby had retired as Bensons' chairman. The journalist and politician Randolph Churchill (1911–1968) lived nearby in East Bergholt and was a more regular visitor to Boxted House; Natalie was the last love of his life.

Just as artists were merely one strand of the remarkable range of people who congregated at Boxted House during the 1950s and 1960s, so fine art was just one aspect of the extraordinary setting in which they gathered. The house reflected the differing characters, but balanced relationship of Bobby and Natalie, giving it its distinctive character. As a result, Bobby's love of classical simplicity could be seen in the fine Georgian furniture which he collected, whilst Natalie introduced colour and energy with highly-decorated textiles and quirky arrangements of shells gathered during trips abroad. Bobby's art historical erudition was reflected in his discerning acquisitions, whilst Natalie's more instinctive response to art was revealed in, for example, pinning a dead goldfinch to a painting of birds by Cedric Morris and draping a necklace around a wooden torso carved by Richard Bedford. The principal rooms were sumptuously decorated, with burgundy flocked wallpaper in the dining-room, while rich lengths of brown and olive velvet were intertwined to create pelmets in the drawing-room. Natalie's 'organised muddles' of papers, photographs and curiosities were piled up on occasional tables and mantelpieces and Bobby's extensive and scholarly library filled many bookshelves. Pug dogs and bantams roamed freely. As Frederick Gore recently recalled:

Entering the house, all the rooms were a delight. Everywhere was colour and comfort, surprises and intriguing treasures. Paintings, interesting ceramics made by Natalie in her studio, which was the grand flowering conservatory full of exotic plants … in the hallway were little Indian elephants hanging on a cord from the ceiling.[42]

The eclectic yet harmonious ensemble was brought alive by Bobby and Natalie themselves; he was the more formal of the two, remembered affectionately for his commanding air, erudition and understated kindness. Natalie was extremely glamorous and brought out the best in people; both had a great talent for friendship and a broad-ranging generosity which, when combined with the gourmet food and wine served at Boxted House, created a warm, memorable atmosphere in the home which was, perhaps, their most significant achievement.

On our last visit … we walked through the garden which had sculptures hidden away in it … towards a great view so that I could paint there … We loved our visits to see Natalie and all the treasures … collected and cherished in that house. It seems like the end of an era.

FREDERICK GORE, 2007[43]

BOBBY died of cancer in 1974. Two memorial exhibitions of his collection were held the following year, at the Minories and at Anthony d'Offay's gallery, whilst the Ashmolean Museum mounted an exhibition of The Bevan Gift and works acquired with the purchase fund Bobby established, as a tribute to their enlightened benefactor.[44] Natalie was also closely involved in the exhibition, *The Bevan Collection*, held at Gainsborough's House in 1978, which included a memorial tribute to the Bevans' great friend, John Nash, who died in 1977.[45]

In 1986 Natalie married Sam Barclay (1920–2000), the sailor and writer, with whom she and Bobby had been friends for years. Sam cared for Natalie selflessly as her memory declined. Following Sam's death in 2000, Boxted House was sold and Natalie moved to a nearby nursing home where she died in 2007, aged ninety-eight.

In its heyday, Boxted House was the distinctive home of a remarkable couple. It housed an important art collection in which virtually every work had a personal link to Bobby and Natalie Bevan, reflecting the achievements of their parents' and their own generation of artists, centred on London before World War Two and in Essex and Suffolk thereafter. The Bevans' hospitality recalled Bobby's parents' 'at homes' of the 1910s and in the 1950s and 1960s Boxted House became the meeting-place for an extraordinary range of people, perhaps only comparable in East Anglia to the circle, of which they were members, centred on Cedric Morris and Lett Haines at nearby Benton End. In its prime, Boxted House, its hosts, contents and visitors encompassed a significant period in modern history, especially the cultural renaissance based in and around Colchester after 1945.

Fig. 20 · Natalie and Bobby Bevan in the 1950s. Private collection

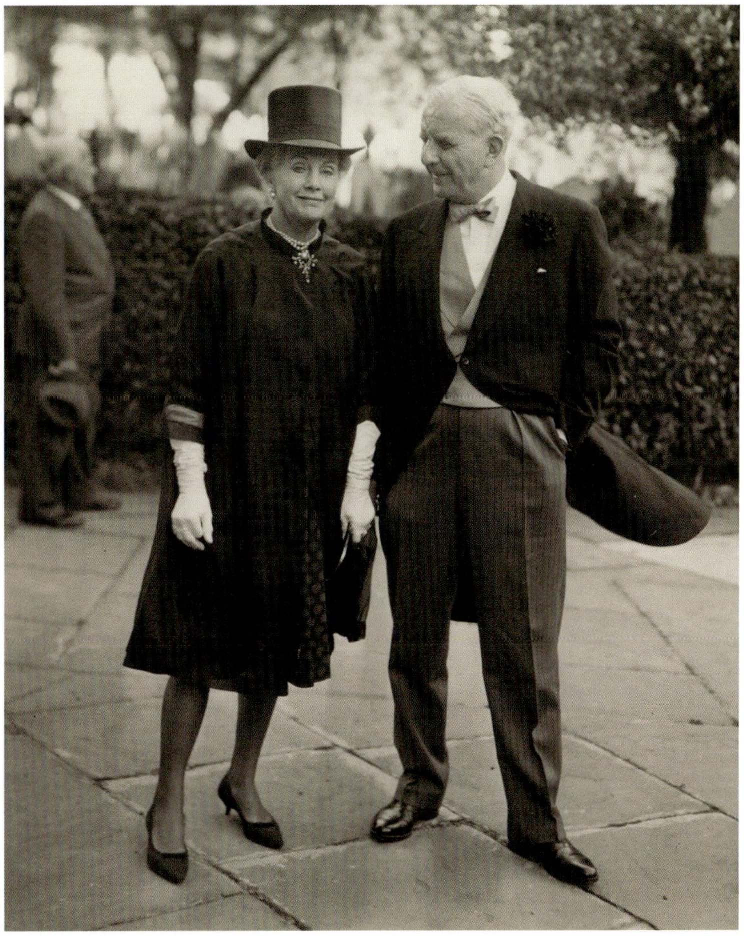

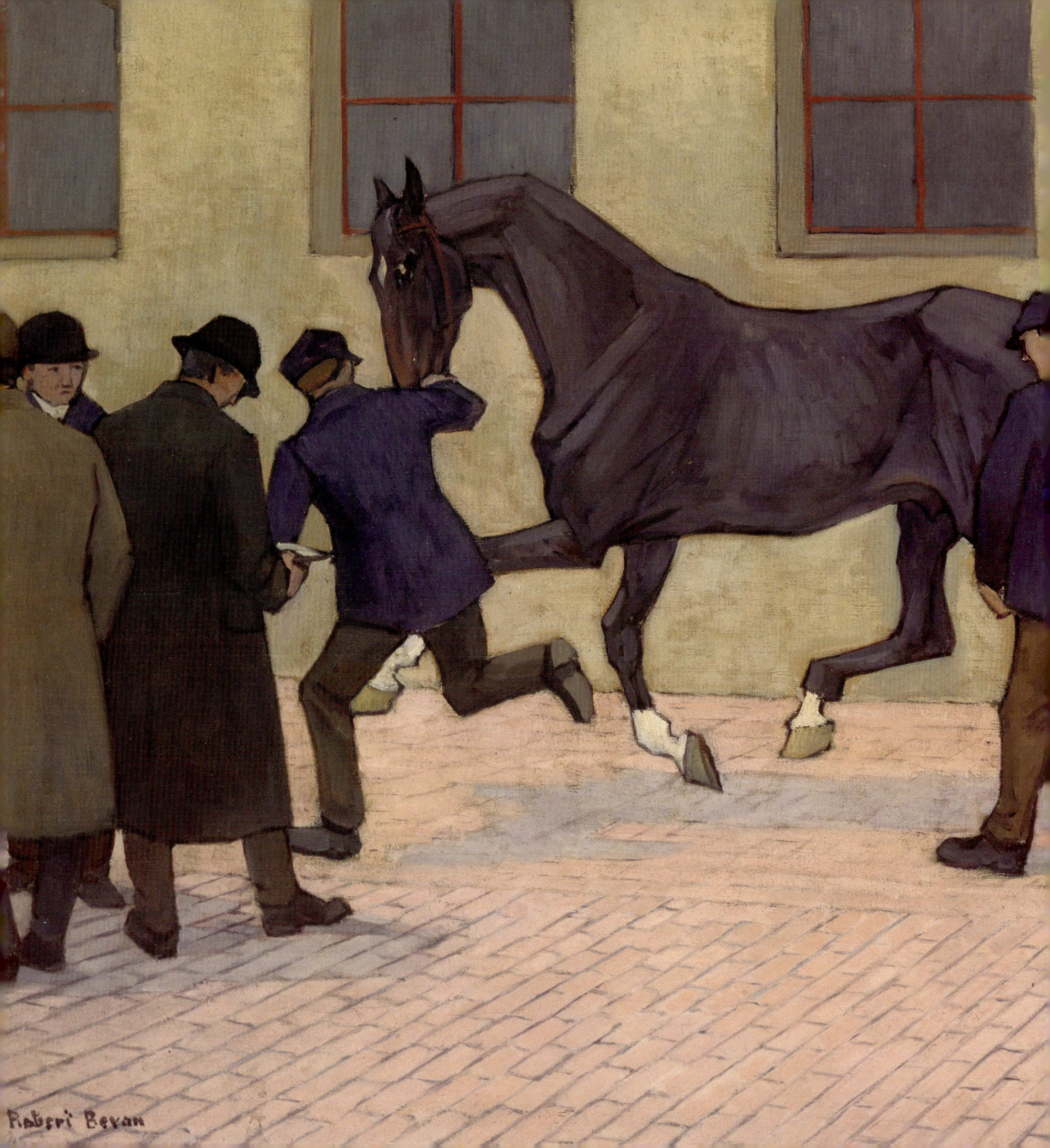
Robert Bevan

Bevan is Good for You: Bobby's Promotion of his Father's Work

FRANCES STENLAKE

BOBBY (Robert Alexander) Bevan was named not only after his artist father, Robert Polhill Bevan, but also after his banker grandfather, Richard Alexander Bevan of Barclays, and his grandfather's business acumen, skipping a generation, appears to have been inherited by him, along with personal ambition and a readiness to apply his qualifications and expertise to appropriate public service. Bobby was born at Horsgate, the large country house built by Richard Bevan as a family home, and was used to staying there with his grandparents. He was almost seventeen years old when his grandfather died in 1918, and so would have been well aware both of the family's long-established identification with Barclays and of Richard's professional and social prominence in the Sussex area. He is also likely to have been sensitive to the fact that his father never earned his own living from his work, let alone enough to keep a family, unlike his two elder brothers, Bobby's uncles, who had followed their father into the bank and become directors of Barclays.

When Robert Bevan died, in 1925, the contrast between his quiet burial in the family plot in Cuckfield, attended only by family and a few friends, and the ceremony which marked Richard's funeral just seven years earlier, cannot have gone unremarked. In 1922, Cuckfield residents had been invited to subscribe to a marble memorial plaque, erected in the church, extolling Richard Bevan's role in the community. Three years later, his son was buried in a coffin simply inscribed 'Robert Polhill Bevan, Artist'.

Bobby's wish to champion his father and establish his reputation at a private as well as public level can easily be understood. He had taken over the marketing of Bevan's work even before his death, and now wasted no time in trying to arrange a memorial exhibition at Goupil's, where Bevan had exhibited since 1911, first with Harold Gilman, Charles Ginner, Edward McKnight Kauffer, John Nash and Christopher Nevinson, then with the London Group, and, most recently, in the annual Goupil Salons of the early 1920s. Bevan's own Cumberland Market Group had held its one and only exhibition here in 1915. Despite this long association, however, the twenty-four-year-old Bobby found that negotiations were protracted. Goupil's being reluctant to take the risk of exhibiting an artist who had never enjoyed commercial success.

Robert Bevan, detail from *Showing at Tattersall's*, 1919 [plate 14]
The Ashmolean Museum, Oxford

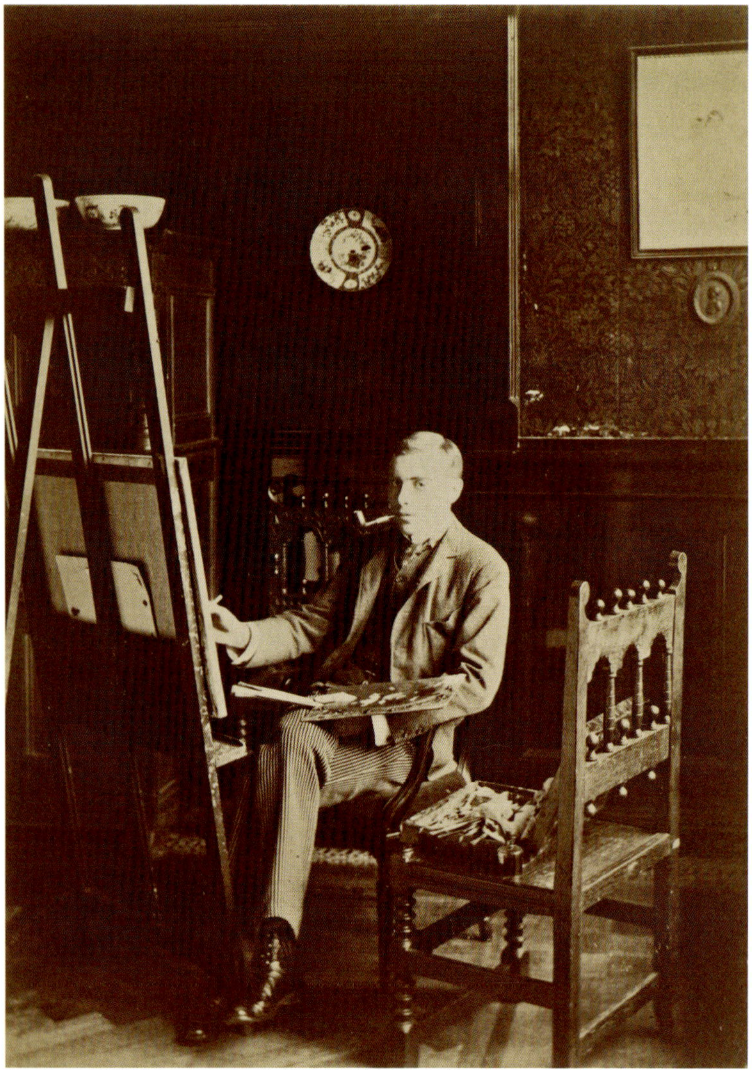

Fig. 21 · Robert Bevan at his easel in the billiard room, Horsgate, *c.*1900. Private collection

Persuading one of his father's colleagues to write an introduction to the exhibition catalogue also took time. Walter Sickert regretfully declined, claiming to be prevented from writing a wholehearted appreciation of Bevan's work by irreconcilable differences of principle.[1] John Nash, mindful of the support he had, as a young artist, received from Bevan, eventually agreed to a task to which he felt ill-suited. However, the favour he asked in return accounts for Bobby's first donation to a public collection: of twenty-seven of Bevan's forty prints to the British Museum, London.[2]

The *Robert Bevan Memorial Exhibition* eventually opened at Goupil's in February 1926 and Bobby found it relatively easy to secure favourable reviews. Frank Rutter, art critic of *The Sunday Times*, and founder, in 1908, of the Allied Artists Association, before becoming director of Leeds Art Gallery, had been a reliably enthusiastic Bevan advocate since 1910, and was now a family friend. His review of the exhibition appeared in *The Sunday Times* of 7 February and an accompanying article, *The Art of Robert Bevan*, was published in that month's *Studio*.

Another ally on whose support Bobby could count was his own friend, Philip Hendy, who had been with him at Westminster School and at Oxford. Hendy subsequently became one of Frank Rutter's successors as director of Leeds Art Gallery, before succeeding Sir Kenneth Clark as director of the National Gallery, London. His review of the exhibition in *The New Statesman* of 13 February 1926 took the form of a detailed commentary on several of the pictures.

A priority was to place more works by Bevan in public collections. During the artist's lifetime, only one painting had been acquired by a public collection: *Cab Yard, Night*, purchased for Brighton Art Gallery from the exhibition *English Post-Impressionists, Cubists and Others* held there in December 1913. In August 1926 Brighton Art Gallery, having selected forty-five works from the Goupil exhibition, held a combined *Robert Bevan Memorial and Professional Photographers' Exhibition* and considered buying two additional Bevan pictures, but these deliberations came to nothing.[3]

It was not until the early 1930s that Bobby made his first sales to public collections and these were in the United States. From 1930 until 1933, while curator of the Department of Paintings at the Museum of Fine Arts in Boston, Philip Hendy purchased a number of Camden Town Group pictures, including two by Bevan. Bobby certainly had friends in the right places but even his skilful 'networking' could be unproductive. During the same period he attempted, without success, to commission a book about his father from the former secretary of the Fitzroy Street Group and the Camden Town Group, J.B. Manson, who had become director of the Tate Gallery, London in 1930.[4]

However, purchases in the United States were soon matched by acquisitions in this country. In preparation for an exhibition to mark the opening of the extension to Liverpool's Walker Art Gallery in October 1933, director Frank Lambert visited Mrs Bevan to select five pictures. His gallery's subsequent acquisition of the horse sale scene, *Under the Hammer*, became the second purchase of a Bevan painting for a British public collection, twenty years after the first. Bevan's largest horse sale subject, *Horse Sale at the Barbican* (Tate Britain) was purchased a few months later under the terms of the Chantrey Bequest, administered by the Royal Academy of Arts, London, an institution that had never accepted a Bevan work for exhibition.

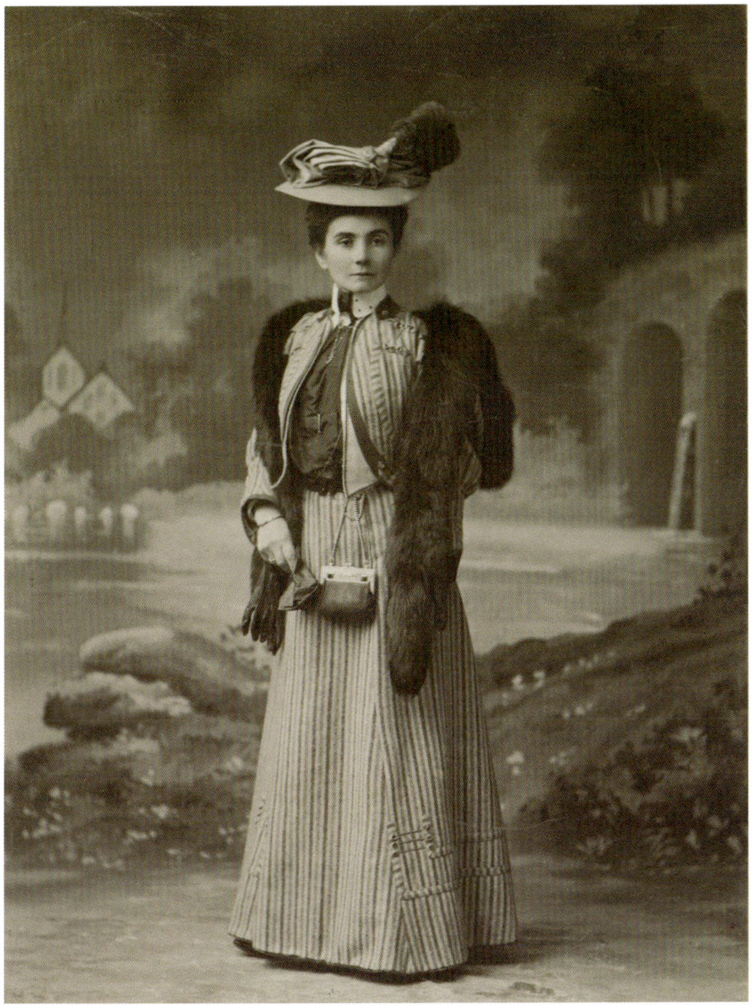

Fig 22 · Stanislawa de Karlowska, *c.*1900
Private collection

For the next twenty years and more, Bobby concentrated mainly on ensuring that his father was represented in as many period exhibitions as possible. His efforts were rewarded by Manchester Art Gallery's purchase in 1935 of *Horse Dealers (Sale at Ward's Repository, no.1)* from the Mayor Gallery's exhibition *Twenty-five Years of British Painting* and by Aberdeen Art Gallery's purchase in 1939 of *Ploughing on the Downs* from a Camden Town exhibition at the Art Exhibitions Bureau. The following year Bobby contributed to the first of the wartime exhibitions in the National Gallery, organised by Lillian Browse, *British Painting since Whistler*, by lending four paintings by his father and one by Gilman. At the same time works were for sale in a Redfern Gallery touring Camden Town Group exhibition.

After the war Bobby resumed his efforts to make sure that Bevan works continued to appear in such exhibitions as the Arts Council's *The Camden Town Group*, in Southampton in 1951, and the 1955 *The Artist and the Café Royal*, held at that favourite rendezvous. Bevan works were included in two Camden Town Group fiftieth anniversary shows in 1961: an Arts Council exhibition of drawings, and an exhibition at the Minories, Colchester, where old friend, artist O'Rorke Dickey, had, in 1957, become the gallery's first curator and John Nash was a governor. In the same year, two oils from Bobby's collection accompanied Brighton's *Cab Yard, Night* to Lisbon for an Arts Council exhibition selected by a committee headed by Philip Hendy.

Meanwhile, Bobby was planning further solo Bevan exhibitions. In 1944, an exhibition of more than forty works, *Paintings by Robert Bevan*, to which Bobby wrote an introduction, was exhibited with drawings by Keith Vaughan at the Lefevre Gallery in Bond Street. A much bigger event was the 1956 Arts Council touring exhibition, organised by John Wood Palmer, of eighty Bevan pictures. The party hosted by Bobby and the glamorous Natalie at the London exhibition attracted useful publicity. Sir John Rothenstein, Director of the Tate Gallery and Sir Philip Hendy, by now Director of the National Gallery, were among the guests.

Another of Bobby's Oxford friends was James Byam Shaw, also the son of an artist, and in 1959 the first exhibition to be devoted to Bevan's watercolours, drawings and lithographs was hosted at Colnaghi's, where Byam Shaw was director. Works were purchased by the Tate Gallery, the Whitworth in Manchester, and the Cecil Higgins in Bedford. Two years later, forty Bevan oils were exhibited at Colnaghi's, Philip Hendy writing the introduction to the catalogue.

In his attempts to secure his father's reputation, Bobby did not think exclusively in terms of sales. The 1957 Bevan Gift to the Ashmolean Museum, Oxford, established the most important public collection of Camden Town Group work in the country. It consisted of Bevan works – four oils, four drawings, eighteen lithographs, and the twenty-seven surviving sketchbooks – and works by Gilman, Ginner, Gore and John Nash. Two further Bevan drawings were added in 1959. Bobby also set up a fund to purchase more Camden Town Group works, and advised as to how this should be spent, thus being responsible for the acquisition of an additional Bevan oil and drawings by Gilman, Gore, Henry Lamb, Wyndham Lewis, Manson, William Ratcliffe and Sickert.

During this period Bobby used his helpful contacts to ensure that articles about his father and reproductions of his work were published in a variety of periodicals, such as *The British Racehorse*.[5] On retiring from Bensons in 1964, however, he could spend even more time on Bevan promotion, and devote himself to marking the centenary of his father's birth the following year. Colnaghi's *Centenary Exhibition of Paintings, Drawings and Lithographs* travelled to the Ashmolean Museum; a third show was held at the Minories in Colchester. To publicise these, John Wood Palmer's appreciation of *The Crayon Drawings of Robert Bevan* was published in *The Connoisseur*.[6] Bobby himself had been busy writing and having more works photographed: later in the year his copiously-illustrated *Robert Bevan: a memoir* was published by Studio Vista [fig.24].

Bobby by no means neglected his mother's work. He had organised, two years after her death in 1952, a memorial exhibition at the Adams Gallery, where she had exhibited in 1935, and in 1968 two major events took place. One was the publication of Graham Dry's catalogue raisonné of the Bevan lithographs, commissioned by Bobby, and promoted by an exhibition of these at the Maltzahn Gallery and Colnaghi's; the other was an exhibition of both parents' work at the Polish Library marking the chairmanship of the Anglo-Polish Society by Bobby's sister, Halszka. Several of the Karlowska paintings exhibited were presented by Bobby and Halszka to public galleries: Aberdeen; the Ashmolean, Oxford; Brighton; Fitzwilliam, Cambridge; Huddersfield; Kelvingrove, Glasgow; Kettering; the Museum of London; Manchester; Southampton; Swindon; Plymouth; the National Museum of Wales and Wakefield. Some of these had already acquired work by Bevan; others made purchases shortly thereafter. Pictures by Karlowska were also presented to the University of Hull and to the municipal collections of York, Nottingham, Worthing and Eastbourne.

From 1966 a series of exhibitions at Anthony d'Offay's gallery of, or including, work by Bevan led to the purchase of several works by public collections, and in 1967 the Mellon Collection began to amass its Bevan holding by purchasing from Agnew's, then from Bevan exhibitions at the Davis Gallery, New York. Sales were made in 1961 to Auckland and in 1969 to Adelaide. In 1958, Bobby presented a picture to the George VI (now Nelson Mandela) Art Gallery in Port Elizabeth, South Africa; when this gallery purchased a Karlowska in 1973, it was given two Bevan lithographs.

It is, perhaps, not too fanciful to suggest that Bobby's strategy of initiating and encouraging the representation of his parents' work in public collections, throughout this country and abroad, can be compared with his grandfather's expansion of the family banking business, in the Brighton and south coast area, by opening a branch of Barclays wherever a railway station was built. Certainly, Bobby's efforts to promote his father, sustained over five decades, resulted in a national recognition of which Richard Alexander Bevan, and his two elder sons, would surely have been proud. Richard was eulogised at the time of his death as 'the father of Cuckfield'; thanks to Bobby he is now recorded beyond this small Sussex town as the father of Robert Polhill Bevan (Artist).

Fig. 23 · Front cover of the catalogue for the exhibition *The Bevan Collection*, held at Gainsborough's House, Sudbury in 1978. This is inscribed by Natalie to her son-in-law, Alan Stewart.
Private collection

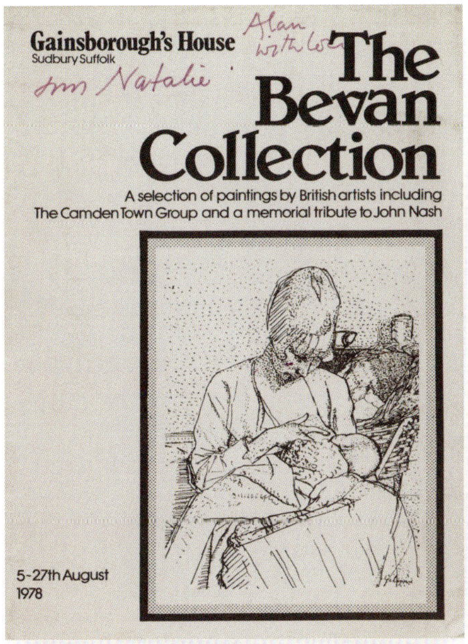

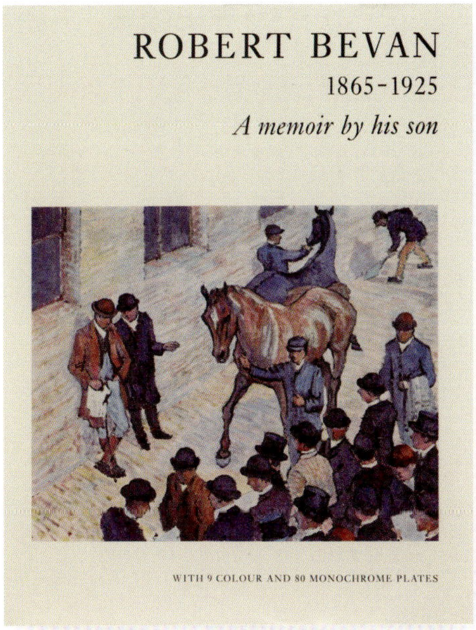

Fig. 24 · Front cover of *Robert Bevan 1865–1925: A memoir by his son*, published by Studio Vista, London, 1965.
Private collection

overleaf Fig. 25
The fireplace in the library at Boxted House.

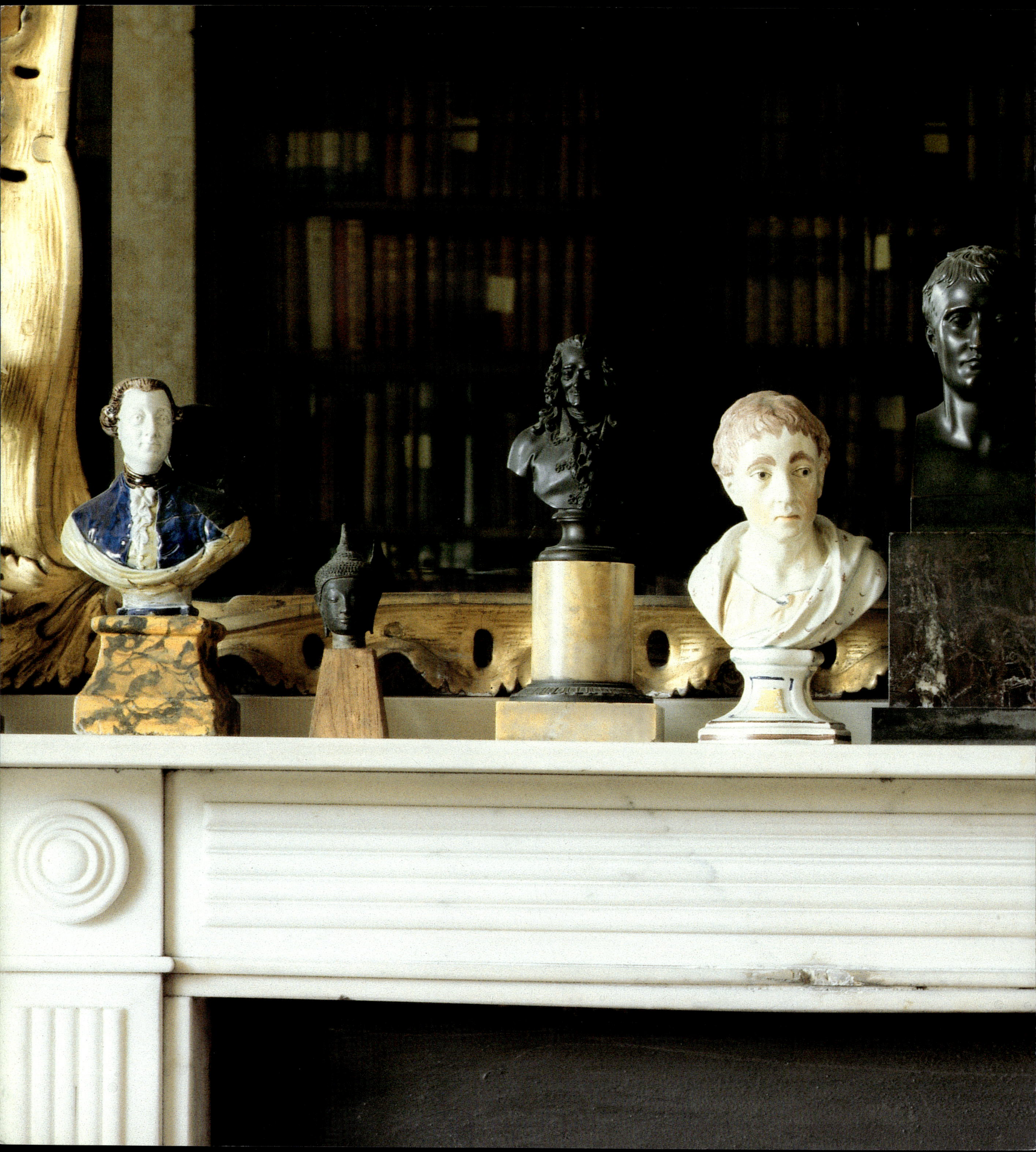

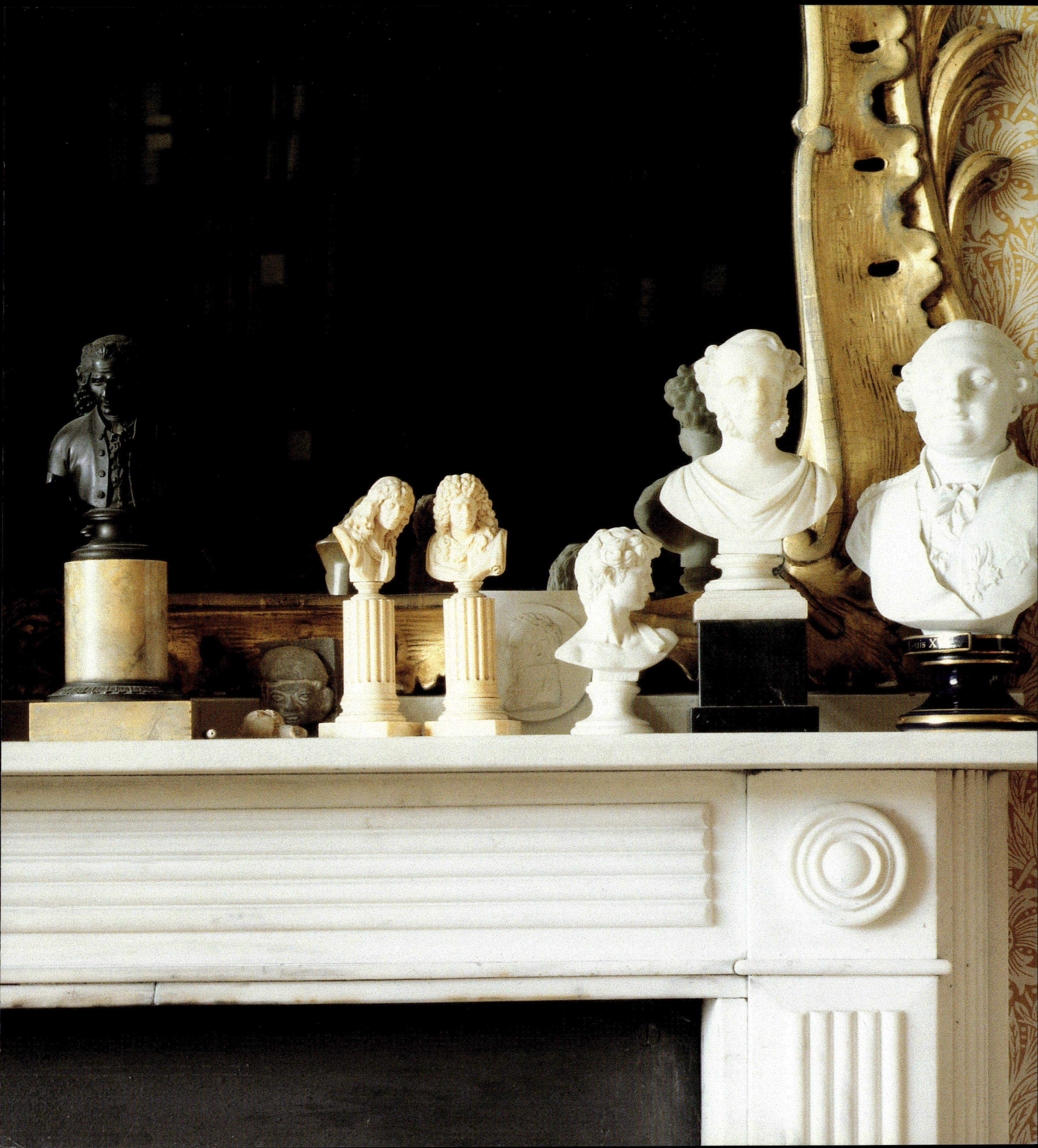

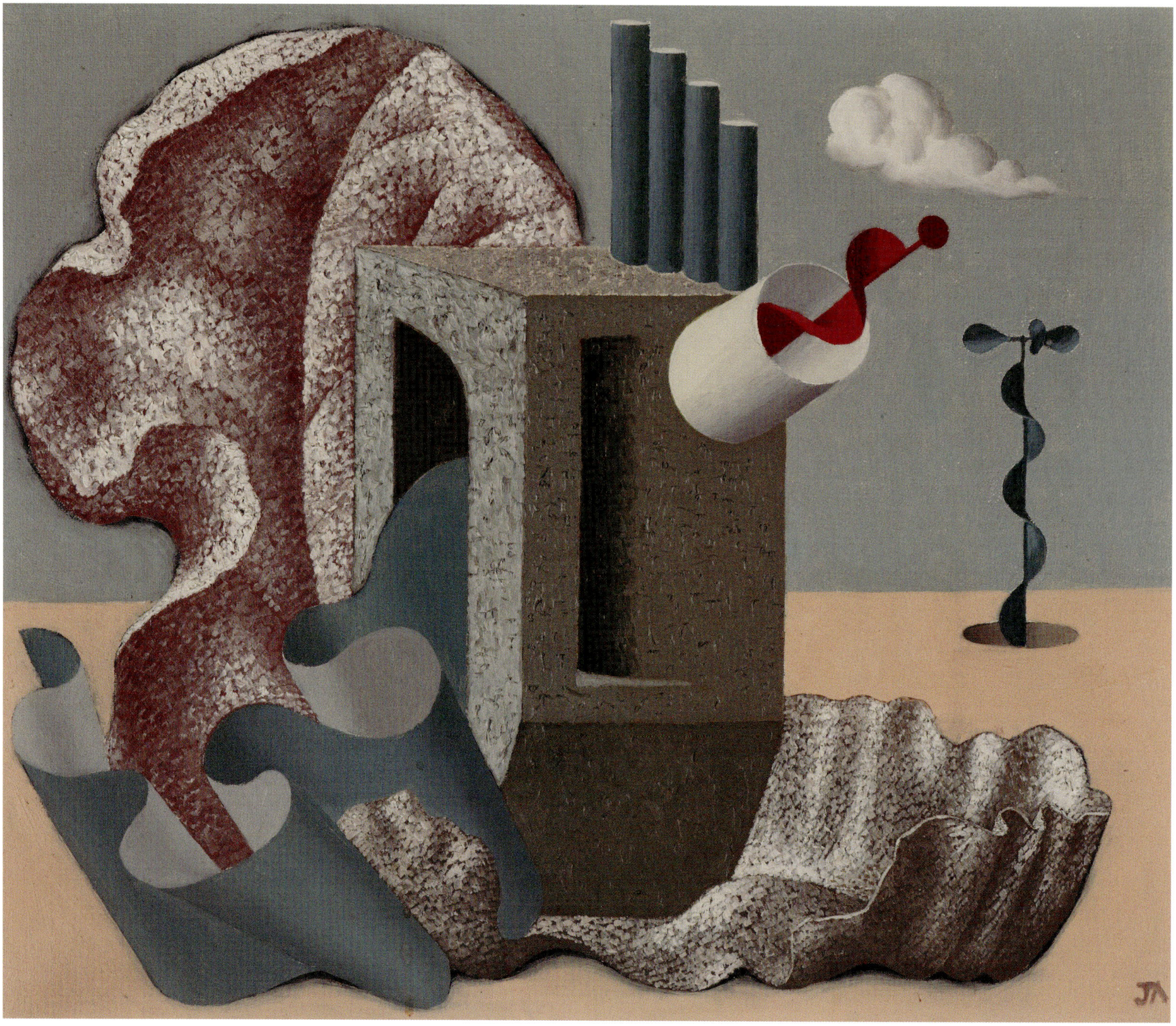

1 · John Armstrong *Velocitor*, 1930–1
Private collection

Natalie Bevan met John Armstrong in London in 1927 and they remained friends until Armstrong's death in 1973. *Velocitor* shows Armstrong's pioneering experimentation with Surrealism; he painted the work several years before the celebrated *International Surrealist Exhibition* was held in London in 1936.

2 · John Armstrong *Still Life with Leeks*, 1955
Private collection

Armstrong painted this work whilst staying at Boxted House over the winter of 1955 and the jug in the painting remains within the Bevan family. It is a good example of the subtle still lifes he painted after World War Two, using a technique of applying short strokes of paint with a square-headed brush.

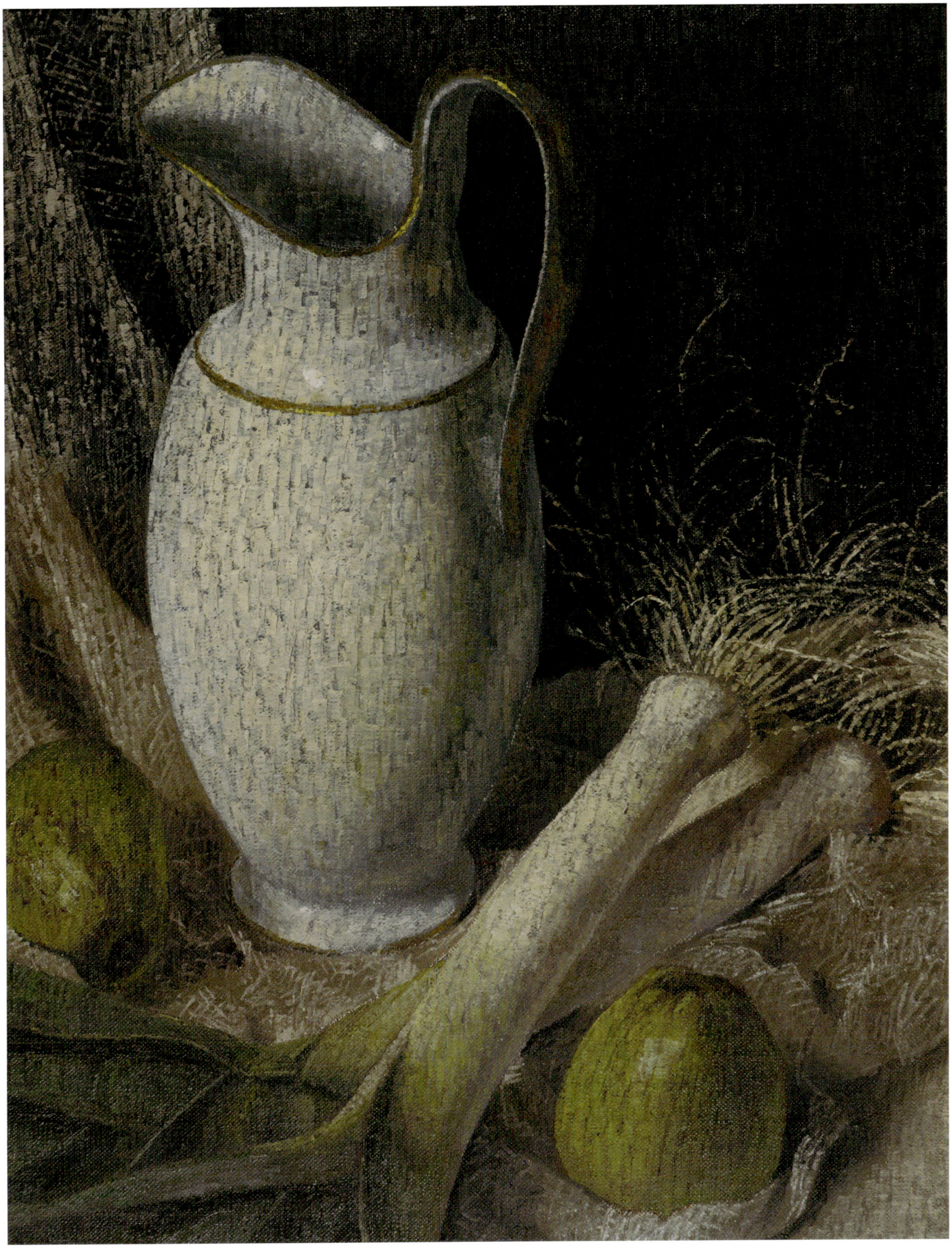

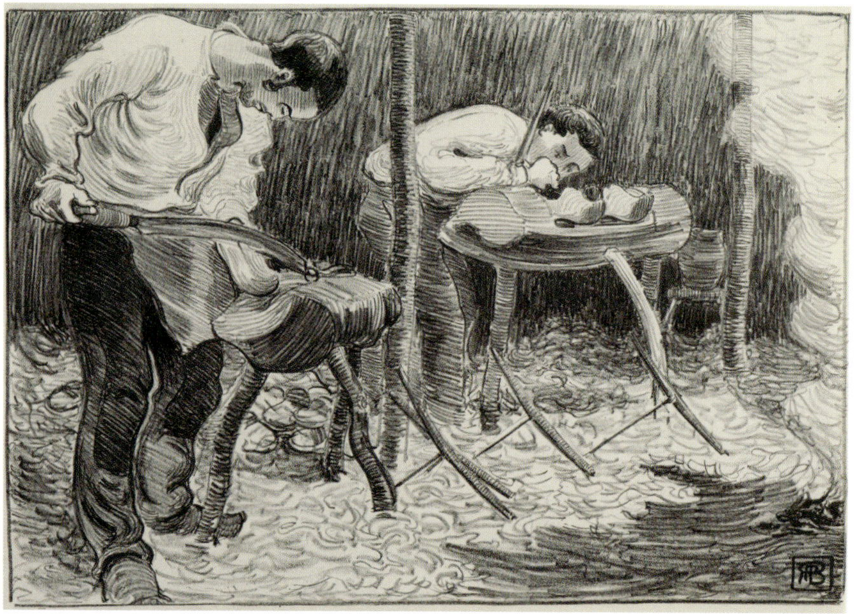

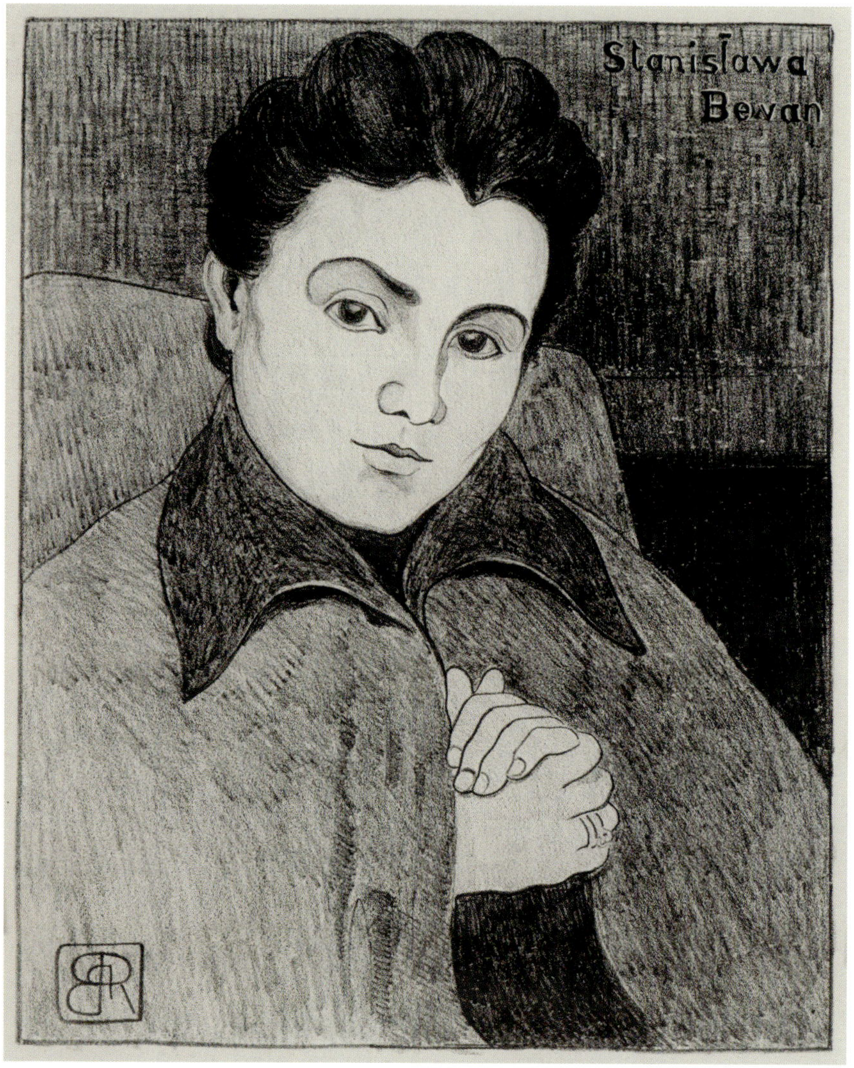

3 · Robert Bevan *Sabot Makers*, *c.* 1892
Private collection

This lithograph was made whilst Robert Bevan was working in Pont-Aven in Brittany. It shows the influence of the Pont-Aven group, which was centred around Paul Gauguin, whom Robert Bevan may have known in 1891 and who he definitely met in 1894. Using strong, curved lines, both the style and the subject – of local Breton craftsmen – also suggest that Bevan was familiar with the work of Vincent van Gogh.

4 · Robert Bevan *The Artist's Wife*, 1898
Private collection

This lithograph depicts Bobby Bevan's mother, the Polish artist Stanislawa de Karlowska, who married Robert Bevan in 1897. As well as sitting for her husband, Karlowska also modelled for other painters in their circle, including Spencer Gore and Harold Gilman.

5 · Robert Bevan
'Found!' from *Four Hunting Scenes*, 1898–9
Private collection

'Found!' comes from a portfolio of four lithographs which reveal Robert Bevan's interest in hunting; a keen huntsman before his marriage, Bevan was Master of the Tangier Hunt from 1892 to 1893 and continued to depict horses throughout his career.

6 · Robert Bevan
The Horse Mart (Barbican no.1), 1920
Private collection

Robert Bevan's depictions of London horse sales held at the Barbican, Aldridge's, Ward's Repository and Tattersall's, are renowned. This lithograph is based on an oil painting of the same title made in 1917–18.

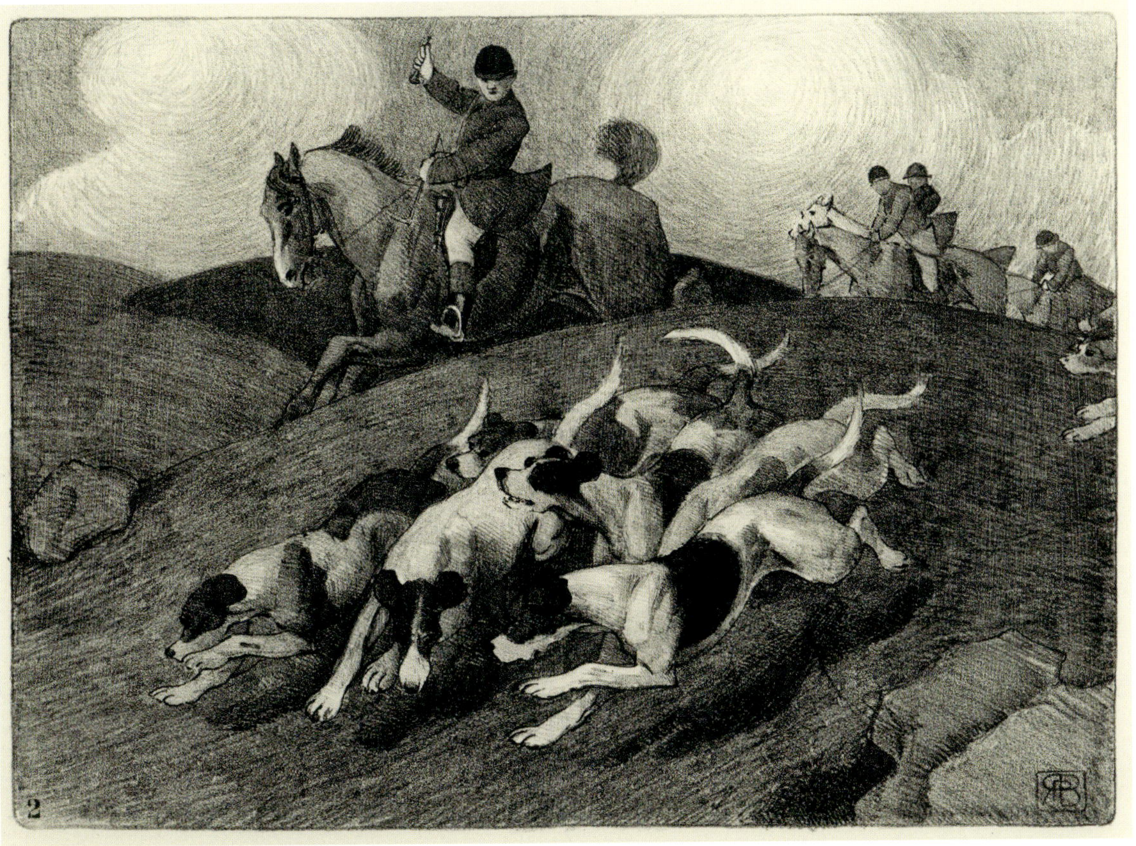

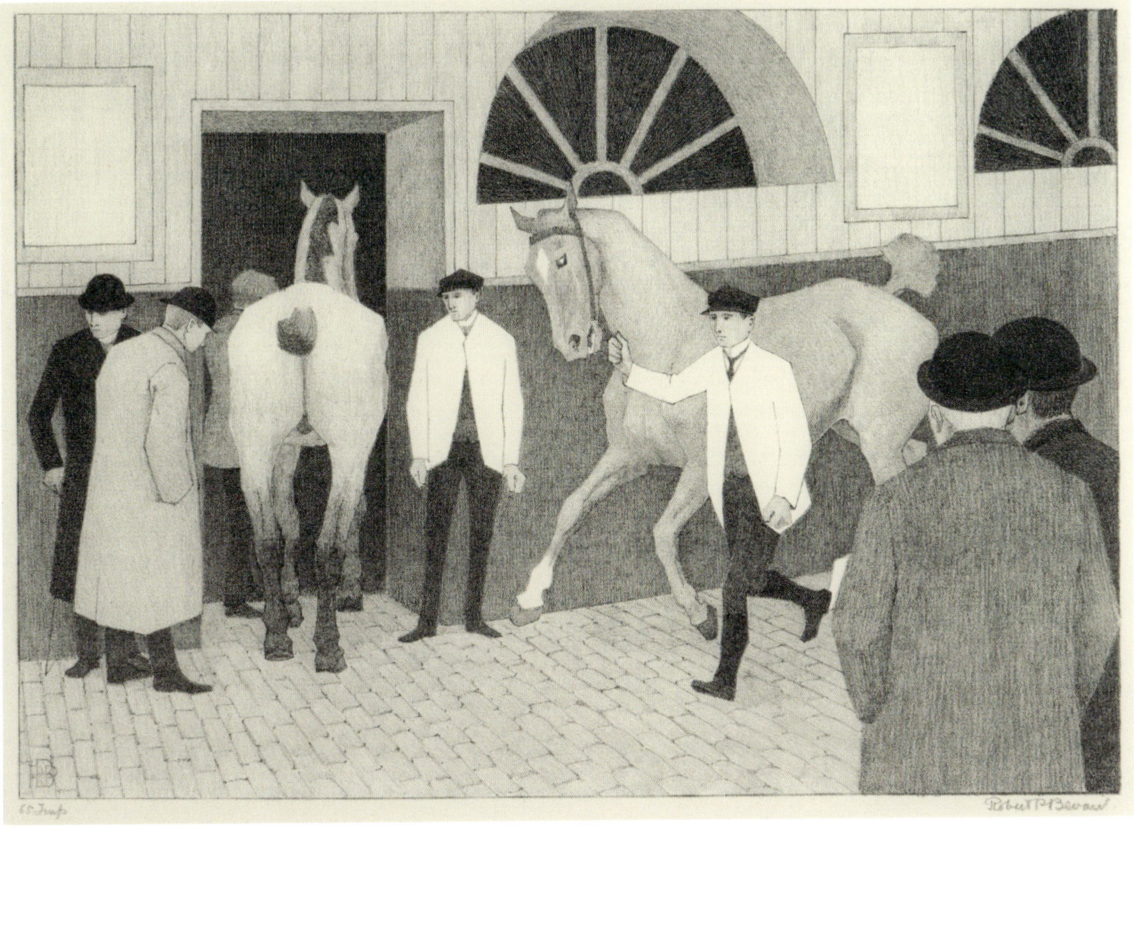

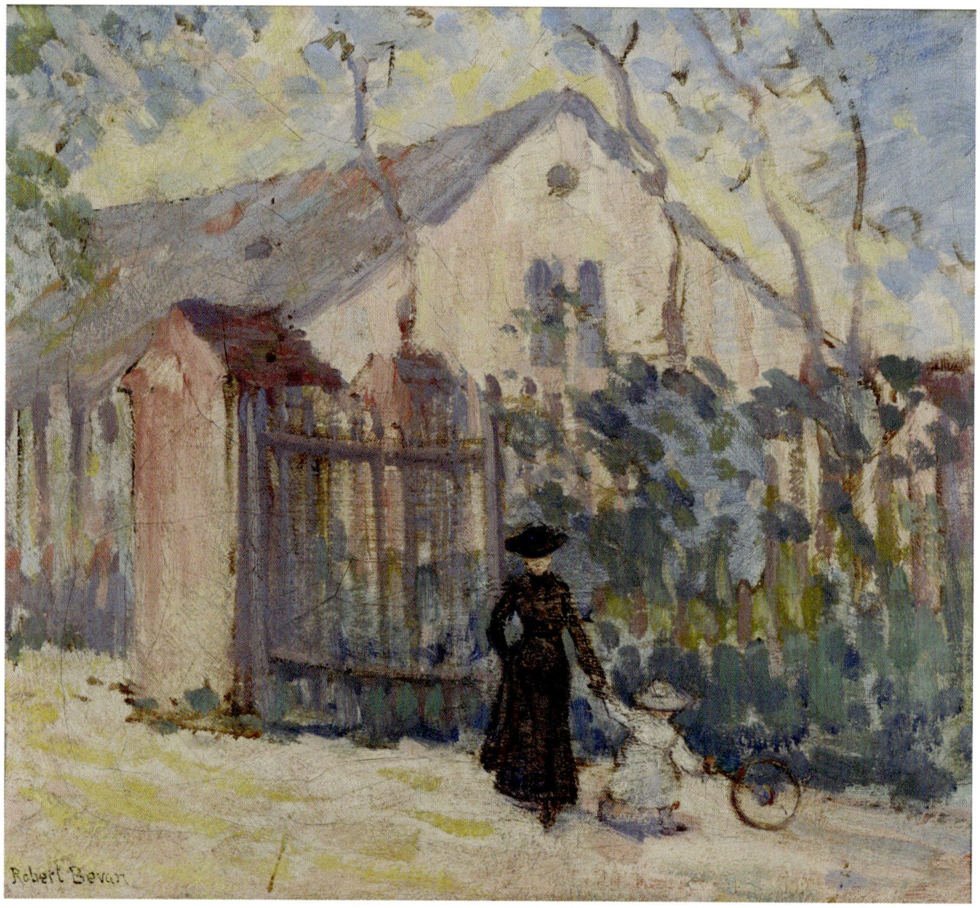

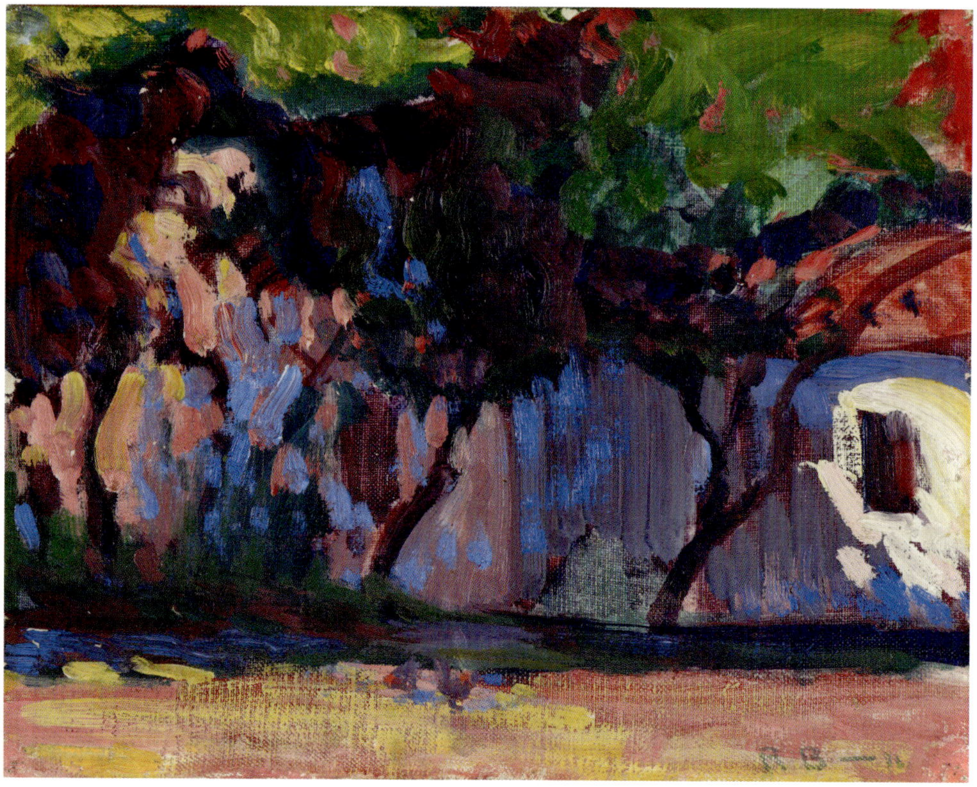

7 · Robert Bevan
The Gate at Szeliwy, 1901
Private collection

This painting depicts Bobby Bevan's mother, Stanislawa de Karlowska, and his sister, Edith (also known as Halszka), during a visit to Poland in 1901. Karlowska's family owned an estate at Szeliwy and the Bevans stayed there during several summers. Small in scale and impressionist in style, Robert Bevan's loose brushwork in this painting contributes to the intimate atmosphere of the scene.

8 · Robert Bevan
Study for 'The Courtyard', *c.*1904
Private collection

This painting is a study for Robert Bevan's infamous *The Courtyard* and both are amongst his boldest and most experimental works. Their blocks of colour and thick brushwork are similar to contemporary paintings of the artists such as Henri Matisse and Andre Derain, who were christened the 'Fauves' when they exhibited at the Salon d'Automne in Paris in 1905. Bevan's *The Courtyard* was savagely attacked by critics when it was shown in his first solo exhibition, held in London in that year.

9 · Robert Bevan
The Artist's Daughter, *c.*1908
Private collection

Bobby Bevan's sister, Edith Halena Bevan, was born in 1898 and was known as Halszka. This is one of the few portraits painted by their father.

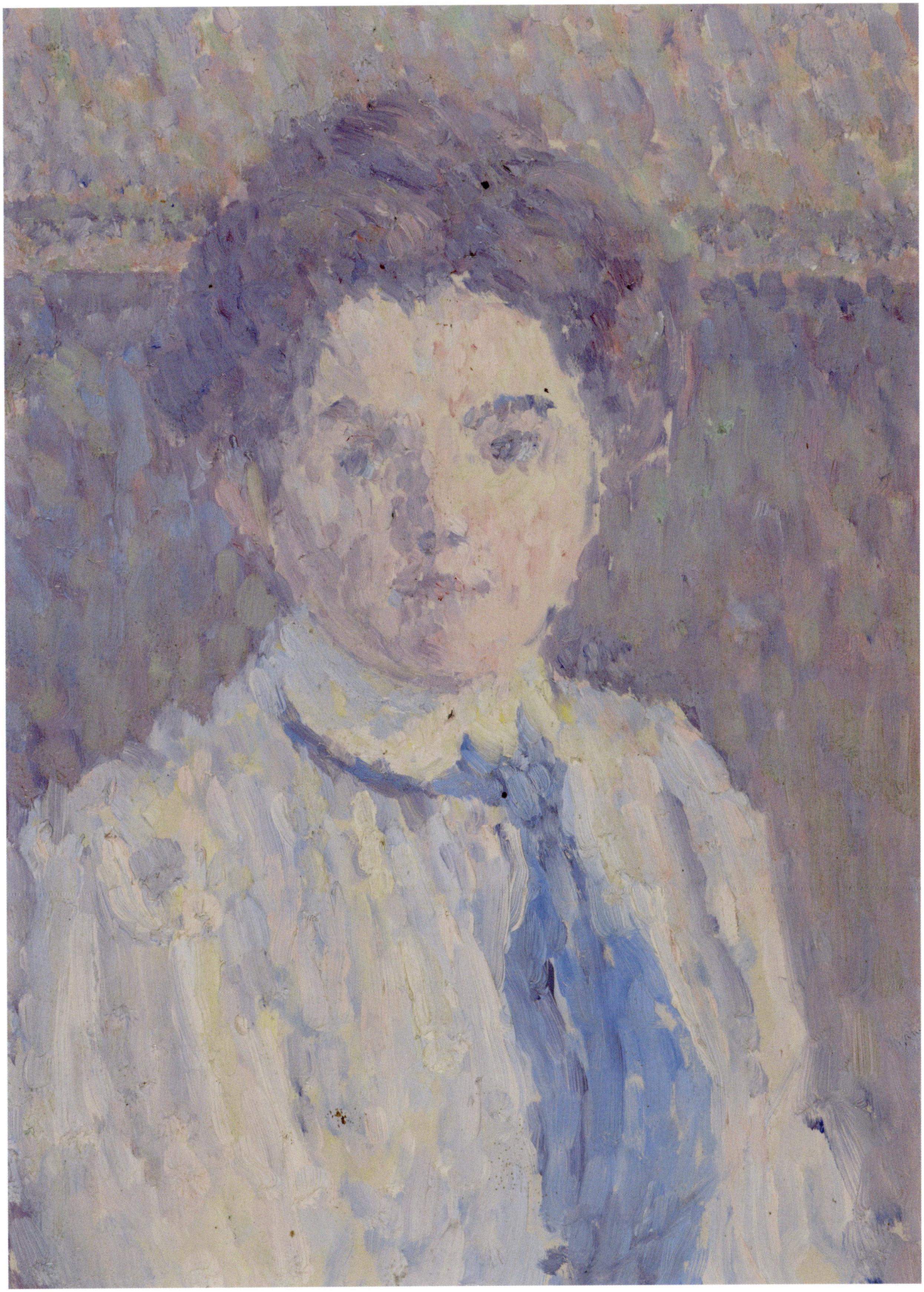

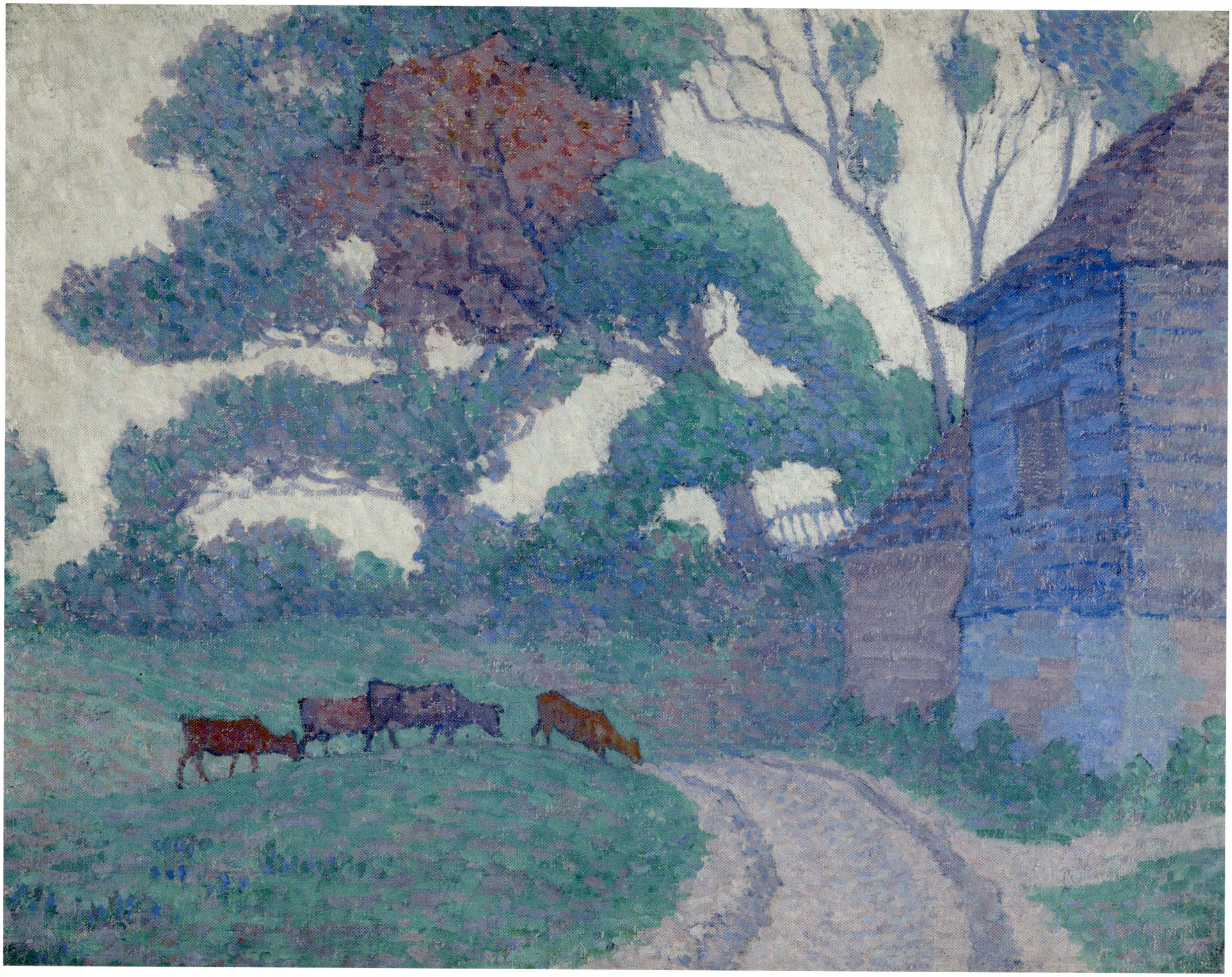

10 · Robert Bevan
*Gravelye Farm, Cuckfield, c.*1911
Private collection

Gravelye Farm was the adjoining property to the Horsgate estate in Cuckfield near Hayward's Heath, where Robert Bevan grew up. This painting shows his interest in Pointillism. The small dots of predominantly green and purple combine to create a tranquil image of the English countryside.

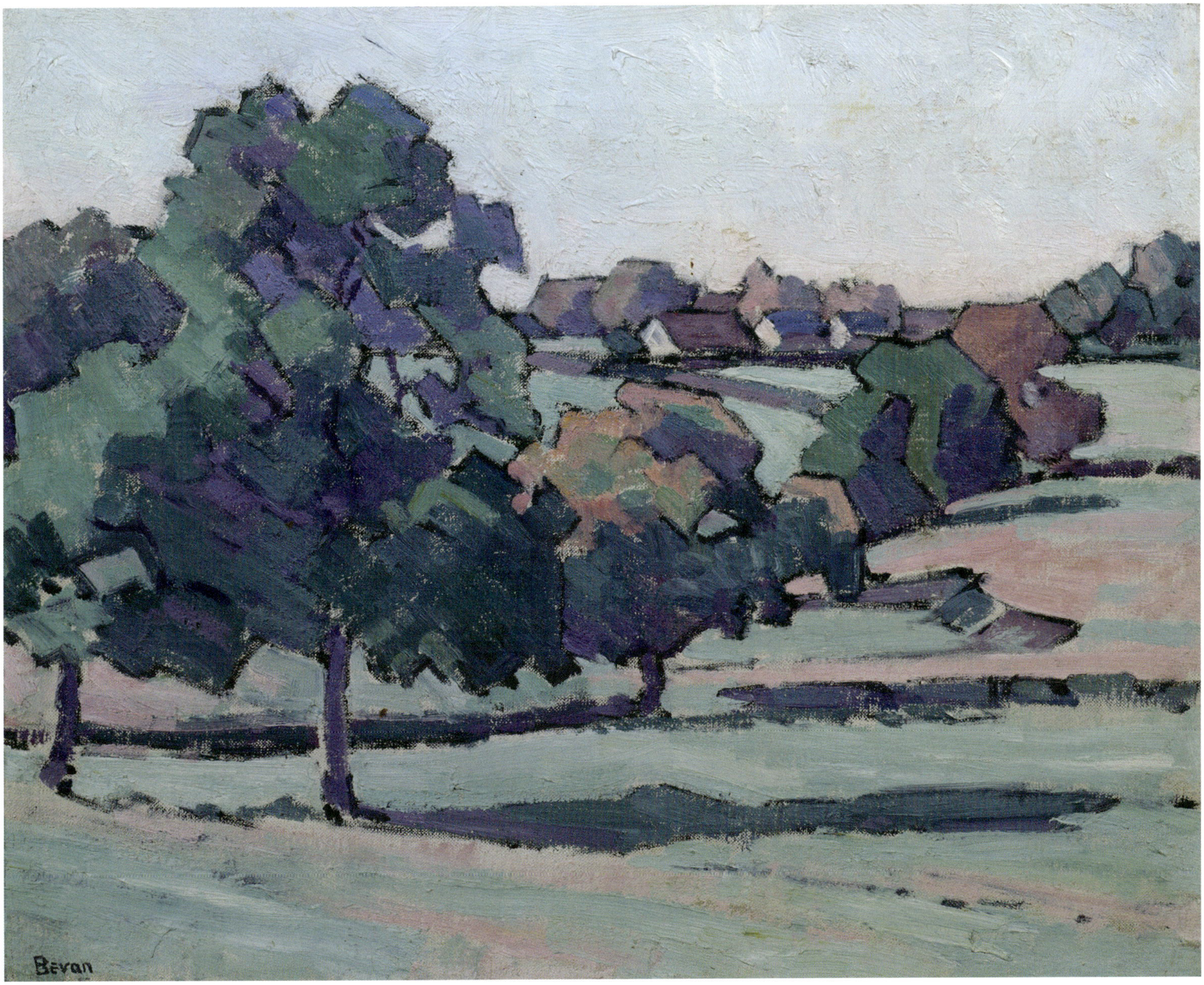

11 · Robert Bevan *Town Field, Horsgate*, *c.*1914
Private collection

Horsgate, near Cuckfield in West Sussex, was Robert Bevan's childhood home. This painting was one of several he made during his final stay there before the house was sold in 1918; it depicts the view looking south-west towards Cuckfield. It is a good example of Bevan's confident handling of paint and emphasis on angular pattern and structure with which he was experimenting at the time. Painted about three years after *Gravelye Farm*, *Town Field*, *Horsgate* shows how Bevan's painting evolved during that period.

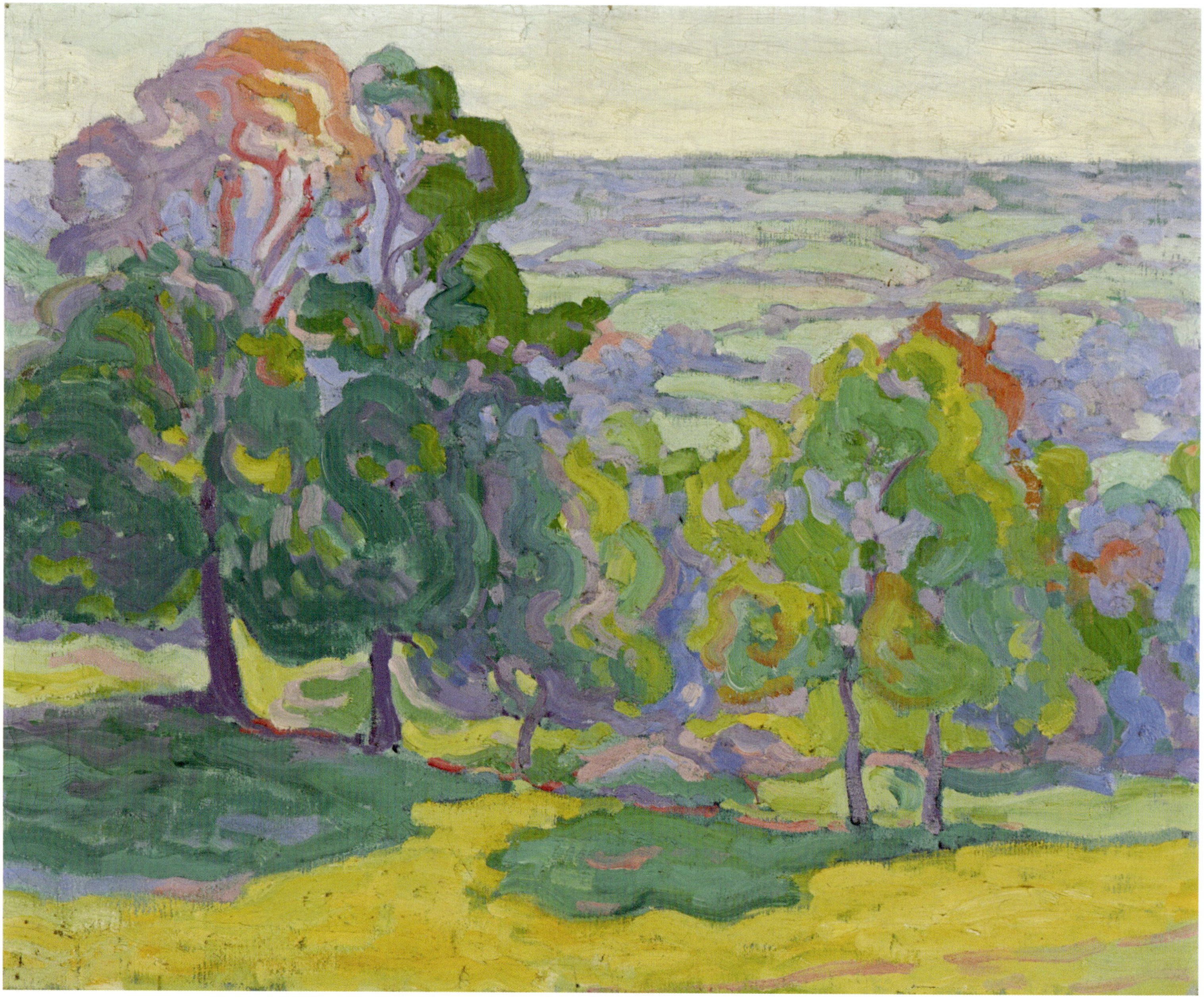

12 · Robert Bevan *Evening in the Culme Valley*, 1912
Private collection

The Culme Valley is situated on the Devon–Somerset border, an area which Robert Bevan particularly liked to paint. The free handling and rich tones of this landscape contrast with works of around the same date, like *Gravelye Farm*, *Cuckfield*, and illustrate Bevan's experimental approach to his work.

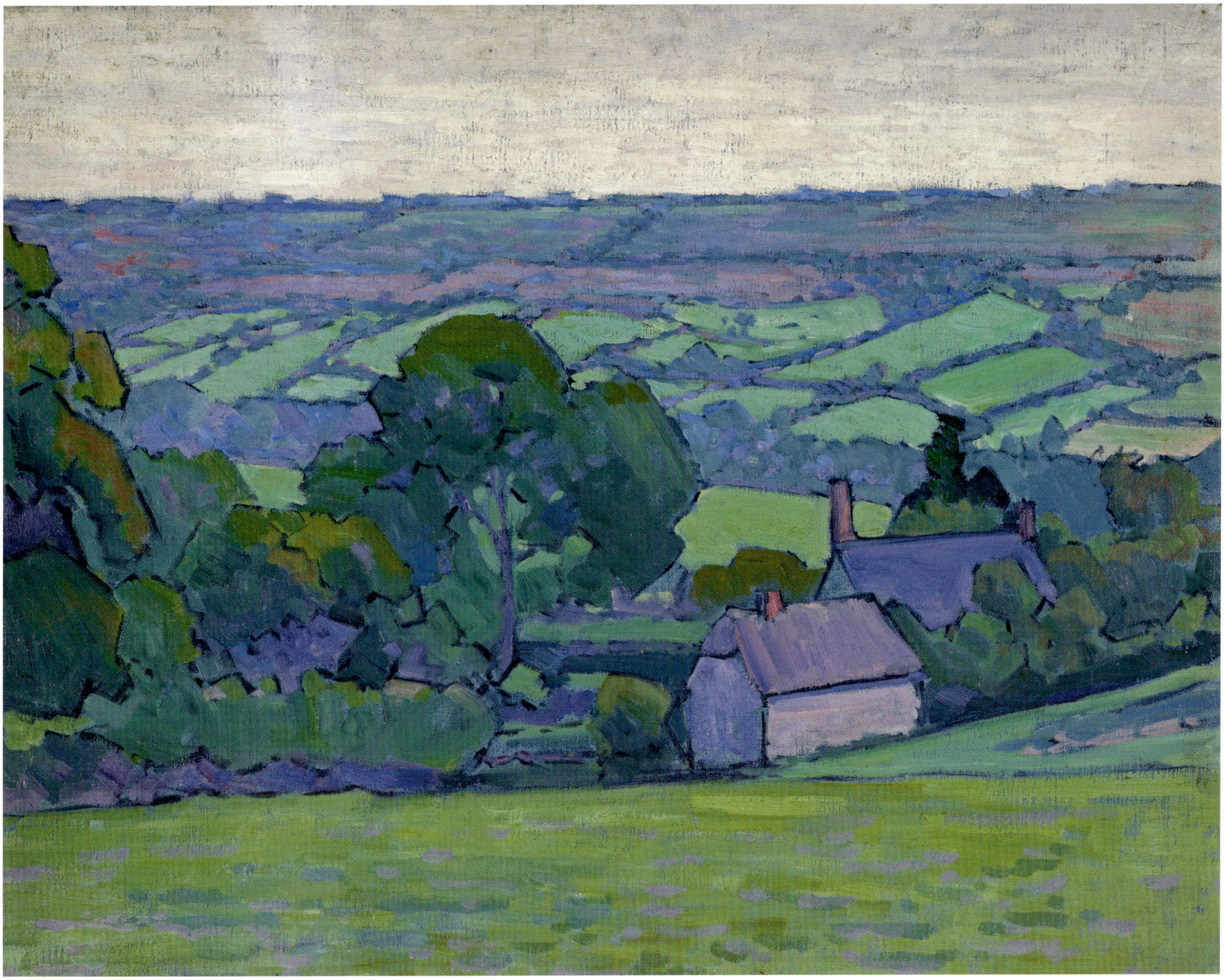

13 · Robert Bevan *A Devonshire Valley no.2*, *c.*1913
Private collection

This painting depicts the back of Dunn's Cottage, not far from Harold Bertram Harrison's farm in Applehayes, near Clayhidon, on the Devon–Somerset border. Frank Dun was Harrison's groom–coachman. Harrison was an amateur painter and ex-rancher and Bevan stayed with him on several occasions in the mid-1910s. The related painting, *A Devonshire Valley, no.1*, *c.*1913 is in the Royal Albert Memorial Museum & Art Gallery, Exeter.

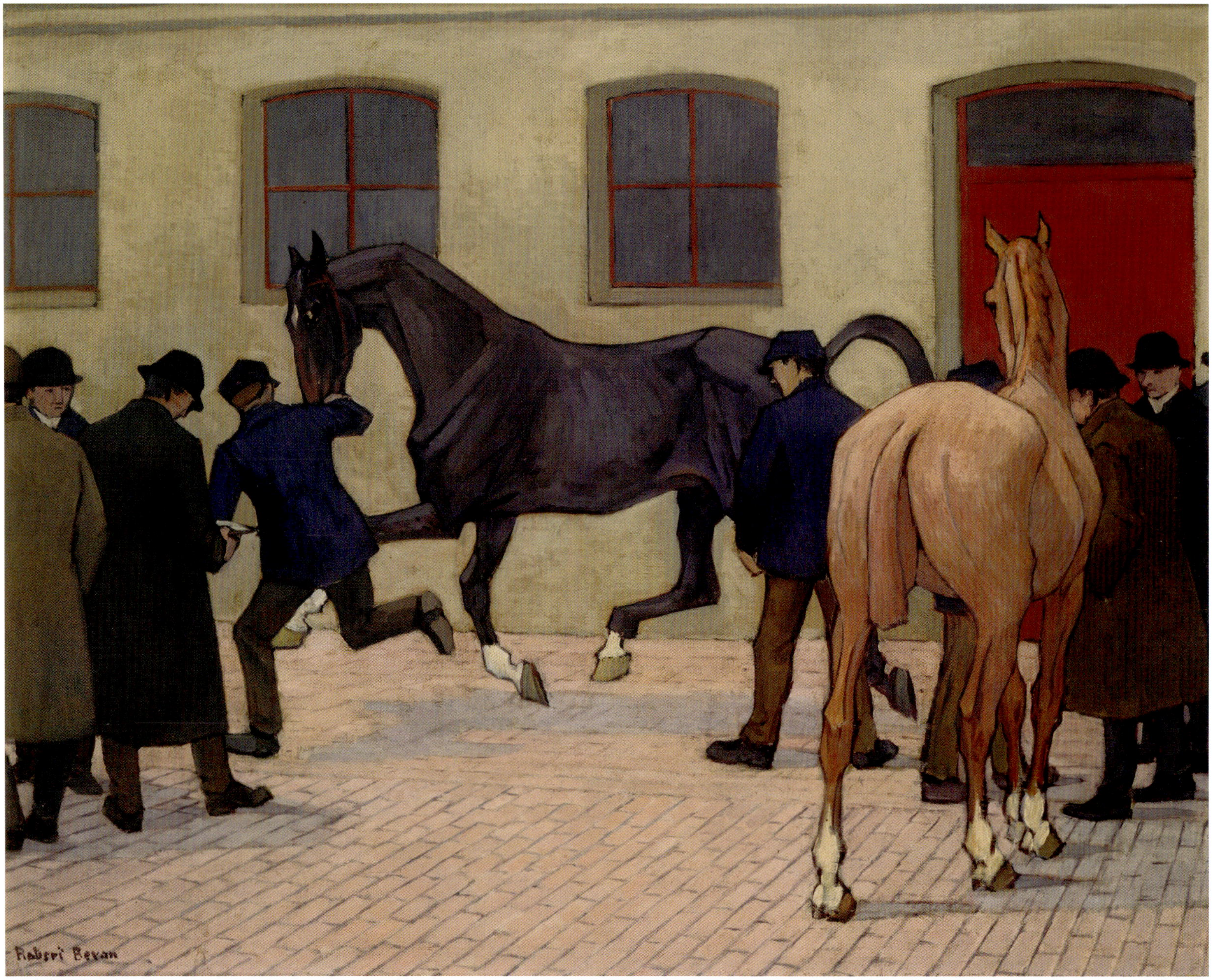

14 · Robert Bevan *Showing at Tattersall's*, 1919
The Ashmolean Museum, Oxford. Presented by R.A. Bevan, the artist's son, 1957.

Showing at Tattersall's is amongst Bevan's most celebrated paintings and was one of the last in his series of works depicting horse sales. Bobby Bevan often accompanied his father to these events, where the artist would draw sketches which he later worked up into paintings in his studio. This is one of an important group of works that Bobby presented to the Ashmolean Museum, Oxford, in 1957 in memory of his father.

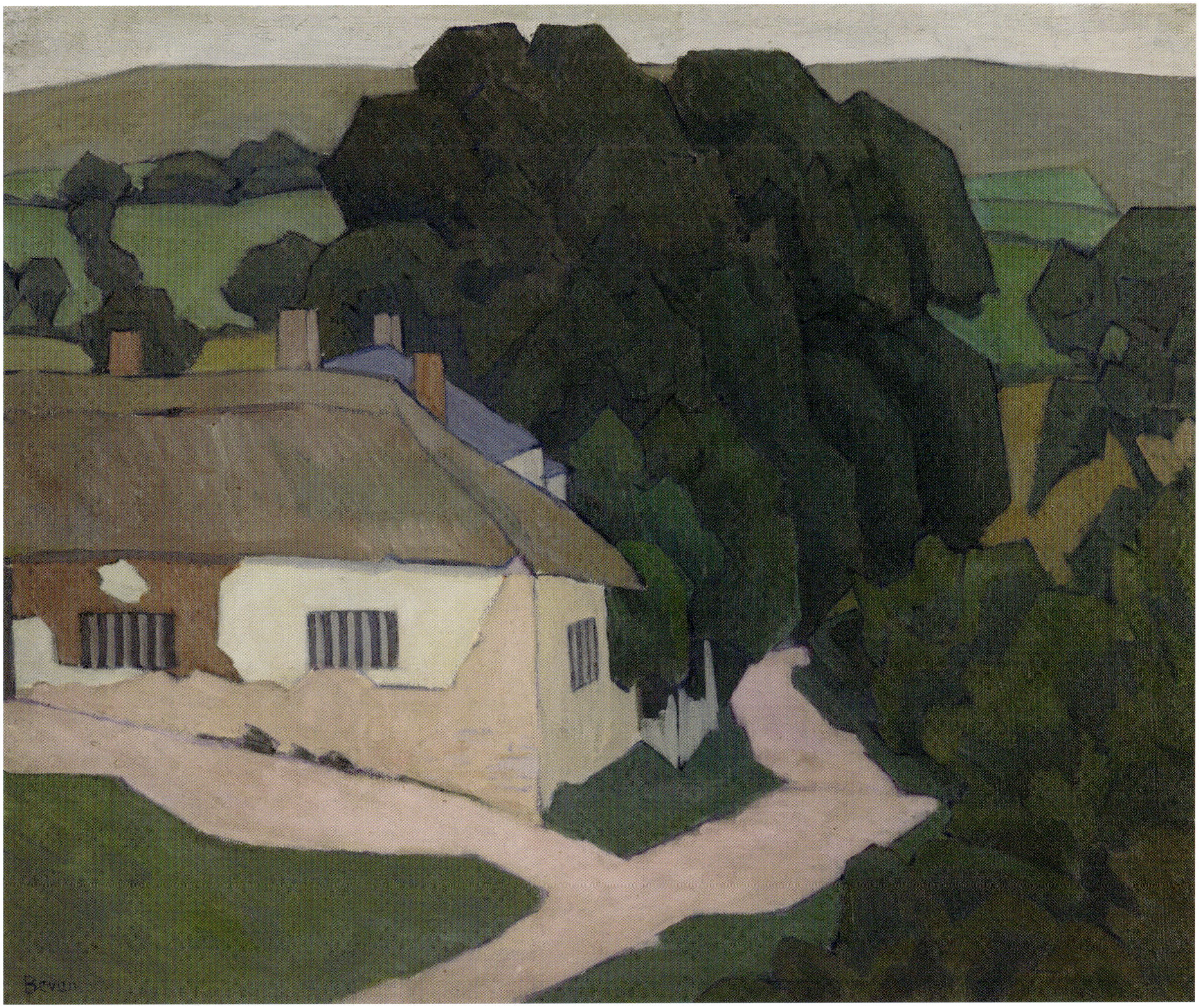

15 · Robert Bevan *The Smithy, Luppitt*, *c.*1920
Private collection

Robert Bevan bought Marlpits, a cottage in Luppitt in south Devon in 1923, where he lived and worked until shortly before his death in 1925. He was already familiar with the area from his visits to Harold Bertram Harrison at nearby Applehayes. *The Smithy, Luppitt* shows Bevan's later style, based on clearly-defined, dense areas of colour, assertive handling of paint and affection for the Devonshire countryside. As he often did, Bevan based a subsequent lithograph on this oil painting.

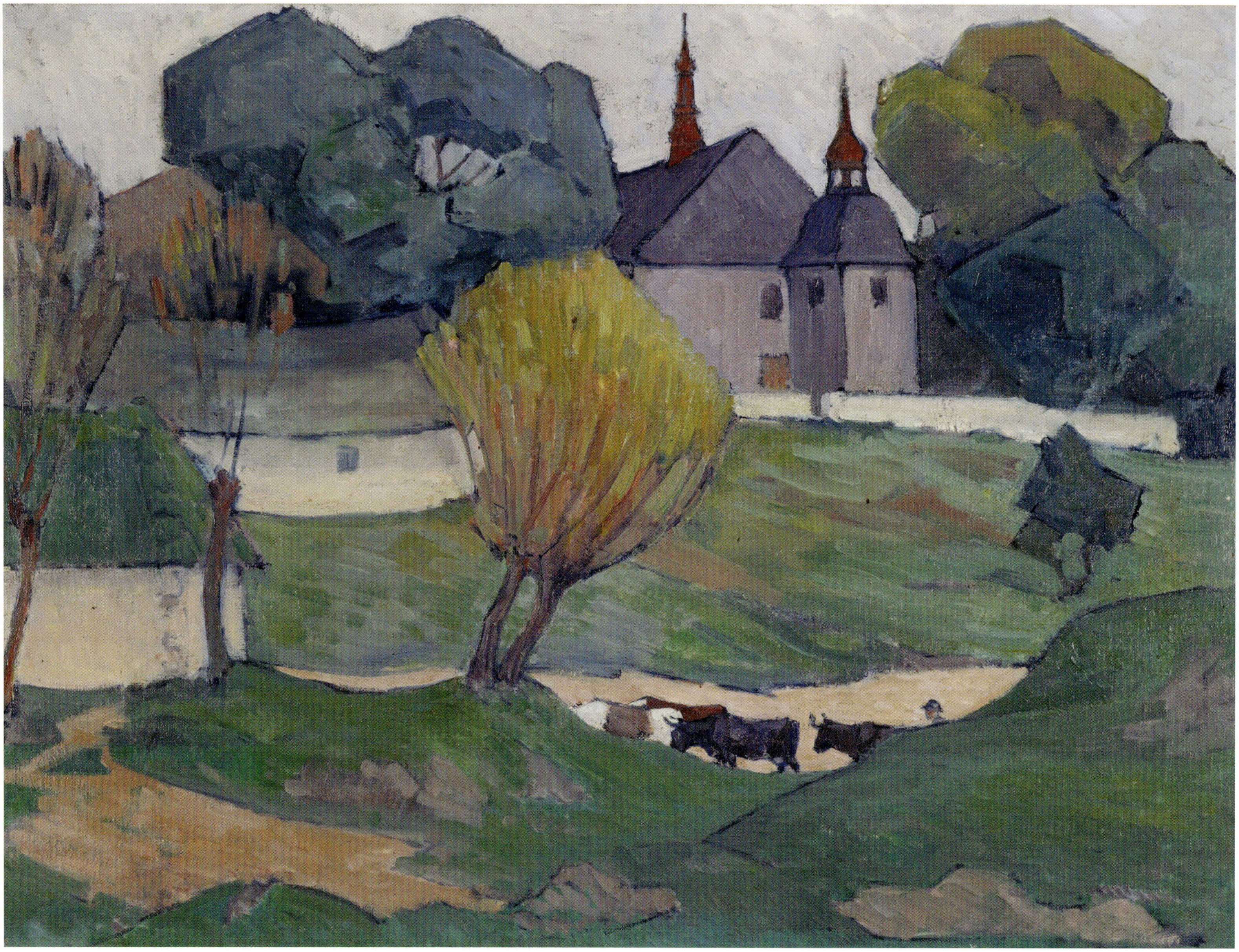

16 · Robert Bevan *A Polish Church, Mydlow*, 1921–2
Private collection

This painting is based on drawings which Robert Bevan made during his final visit to his wife's native Poland in 1921. The motif of the cows being herded in the middle distance can be seen in the related watercolour and crayon drawing *Cows and Cowherd*, which also hung at Boxted House.

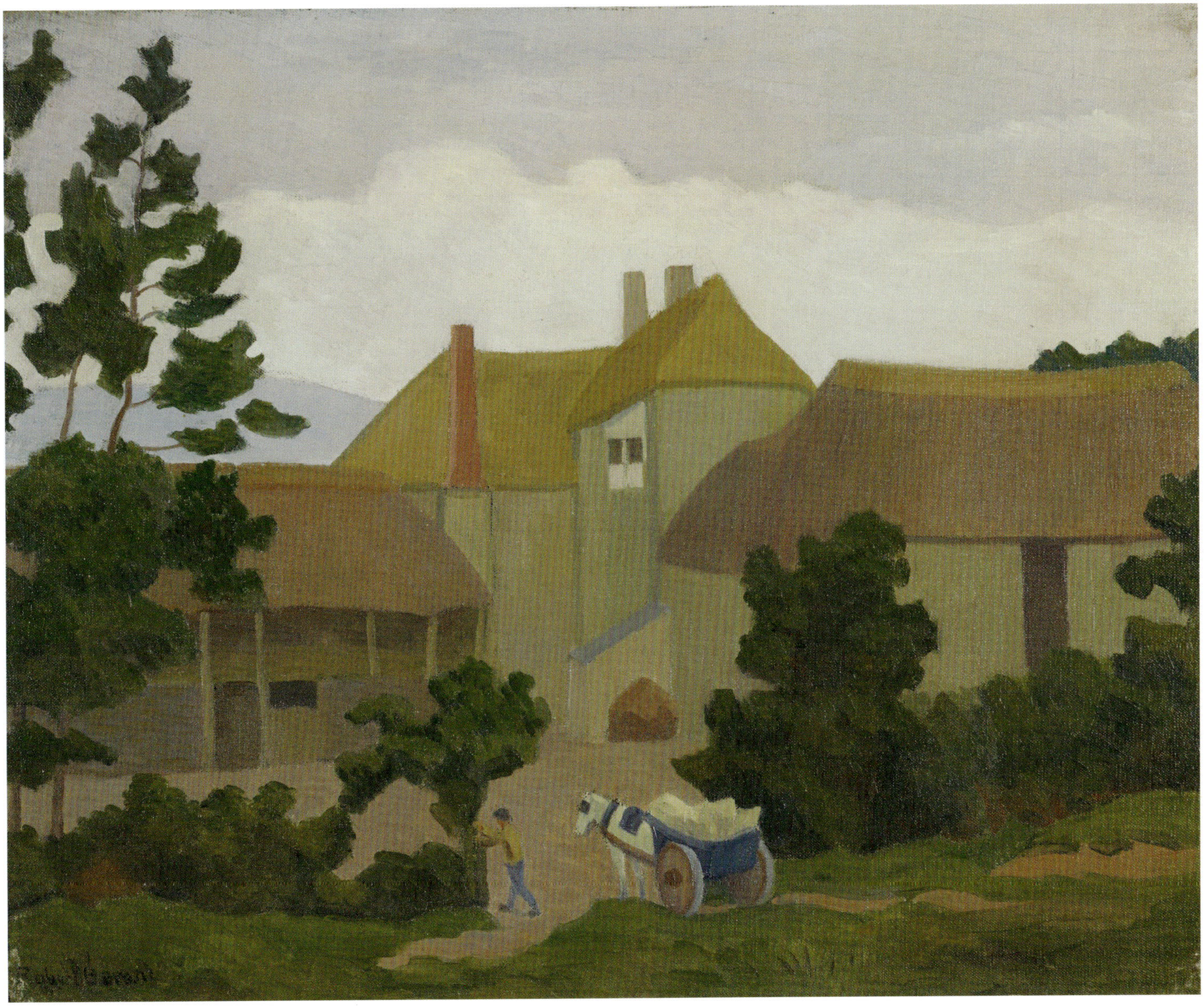

17 · Robert Bevan *Stoneacre Farm no. 2*, 1924
Private collection

From 1923 until his death in 1925, the year after he painted *Stoneacre Farm no. 2*, Bevan was based in a cottage at Luppitt in Devon. This painting is one of three which Bevan made of a local farm and shows the freer, more relaxed style of his late work and his continued interest in rural architecture.

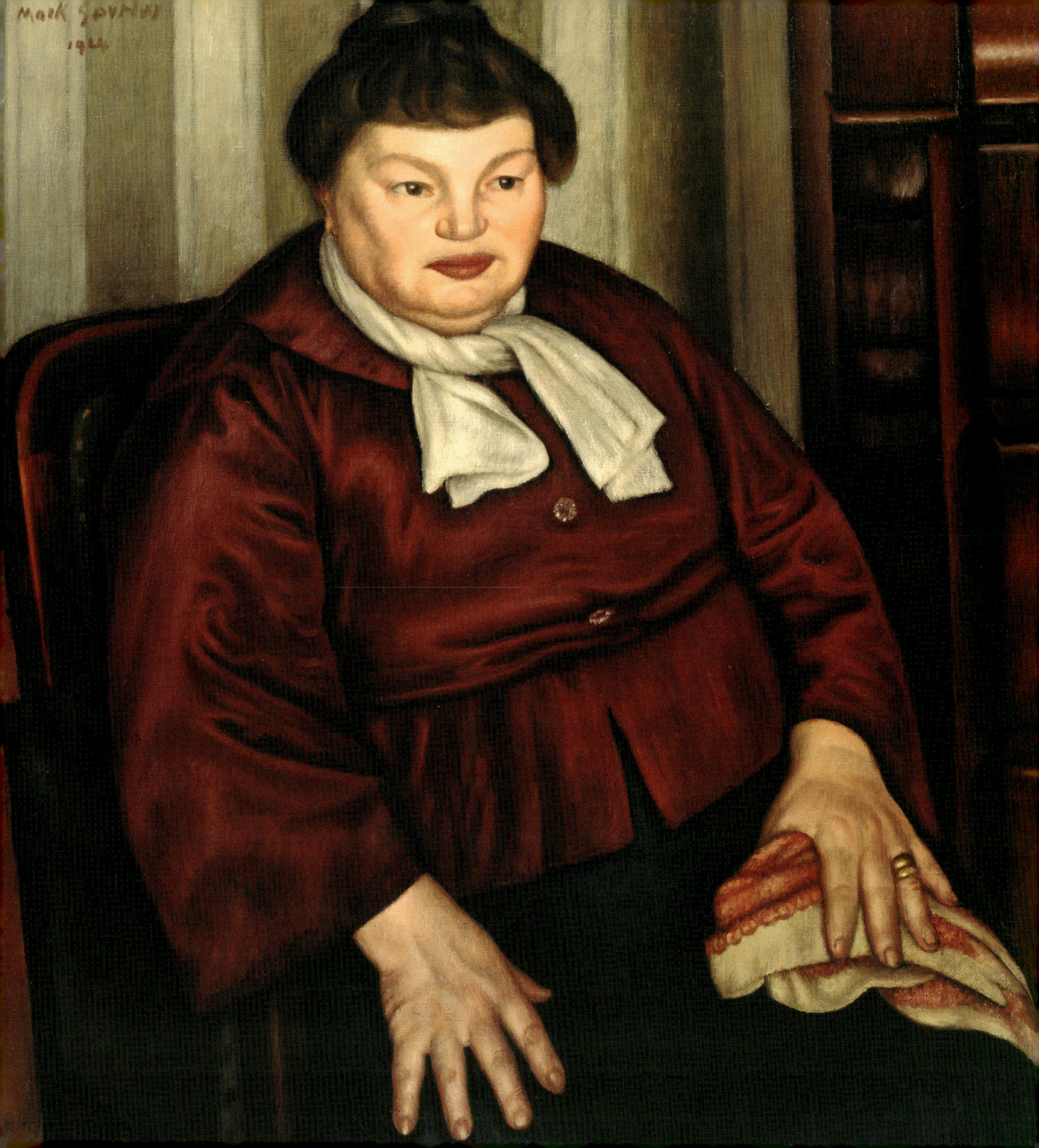
Mark Gertler
1924

18 · Mark Gertler
Portrait of the Artist's Mother, 1924
Private collection

Bobby Bevan purchased *Portrait of the Artist's Mother* in 1956 for the advertising agency S.H. Benson Ltd. Bobby worked at Bensons from 1923 until his retirement in 1964, when he was presented with this painting. It was Mark Gertler's final portrait of his mother and it sold shortly after he painted it for £200, the highest price any of his works fetched during his lifetime.

19 · Mark Gertler
Supper (Natalie Denny), 1928
Private collection

Natalie Bevan (née Denny) met Mark Gertler at a New Year's party held by Augustus John, in 1927, when she was eighteen years old. Gertler immediately asked her to model for him and she sat for two portraits, including the sensual *Supper*. At first glance, the image appears to be one of rich abundance, but in fact Natalie's 'fur' is a blanket, her 'gown' is a slip and the 'linen' tablecloth was a tea towel. This painting was hung in pride of place at Boxted House.

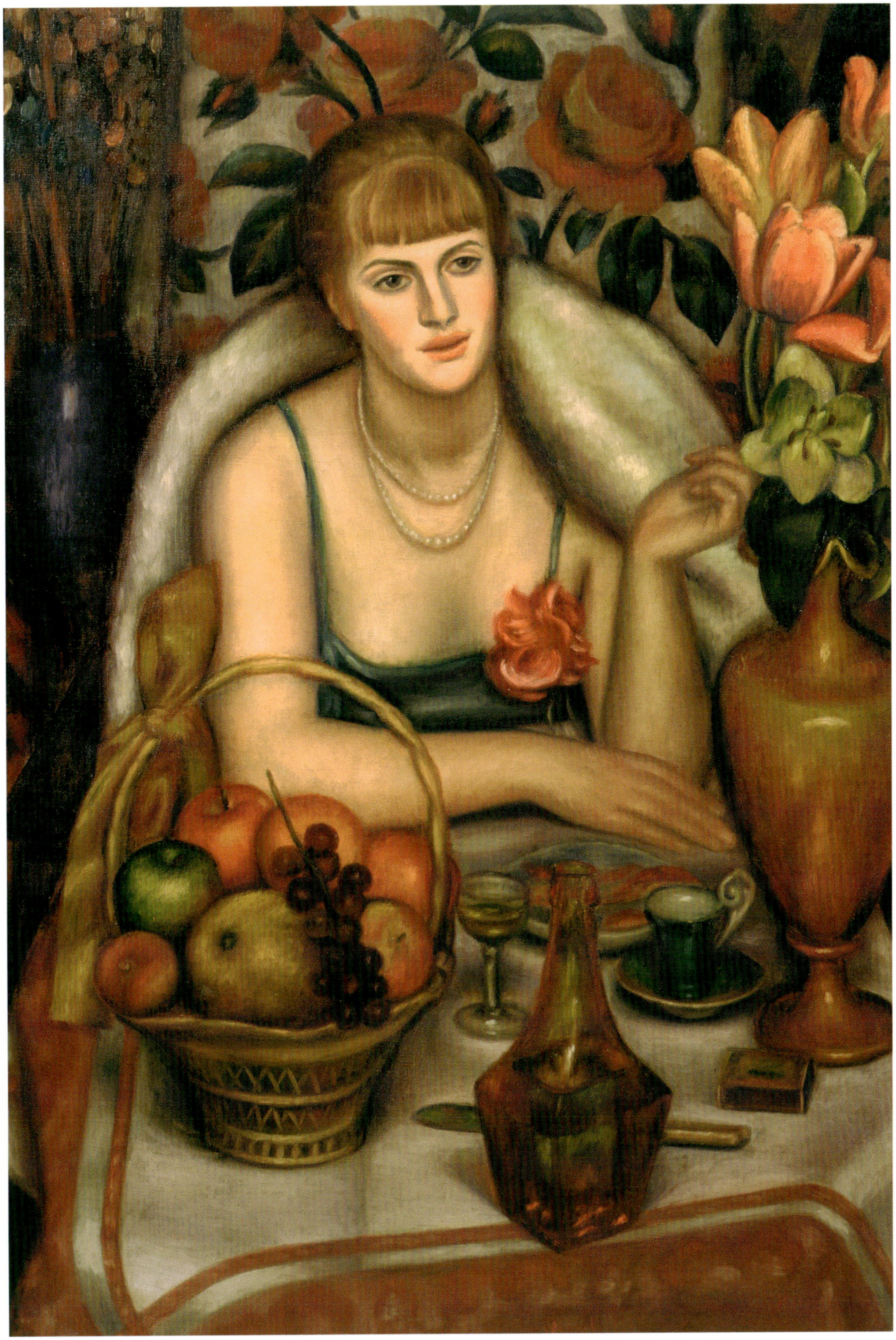

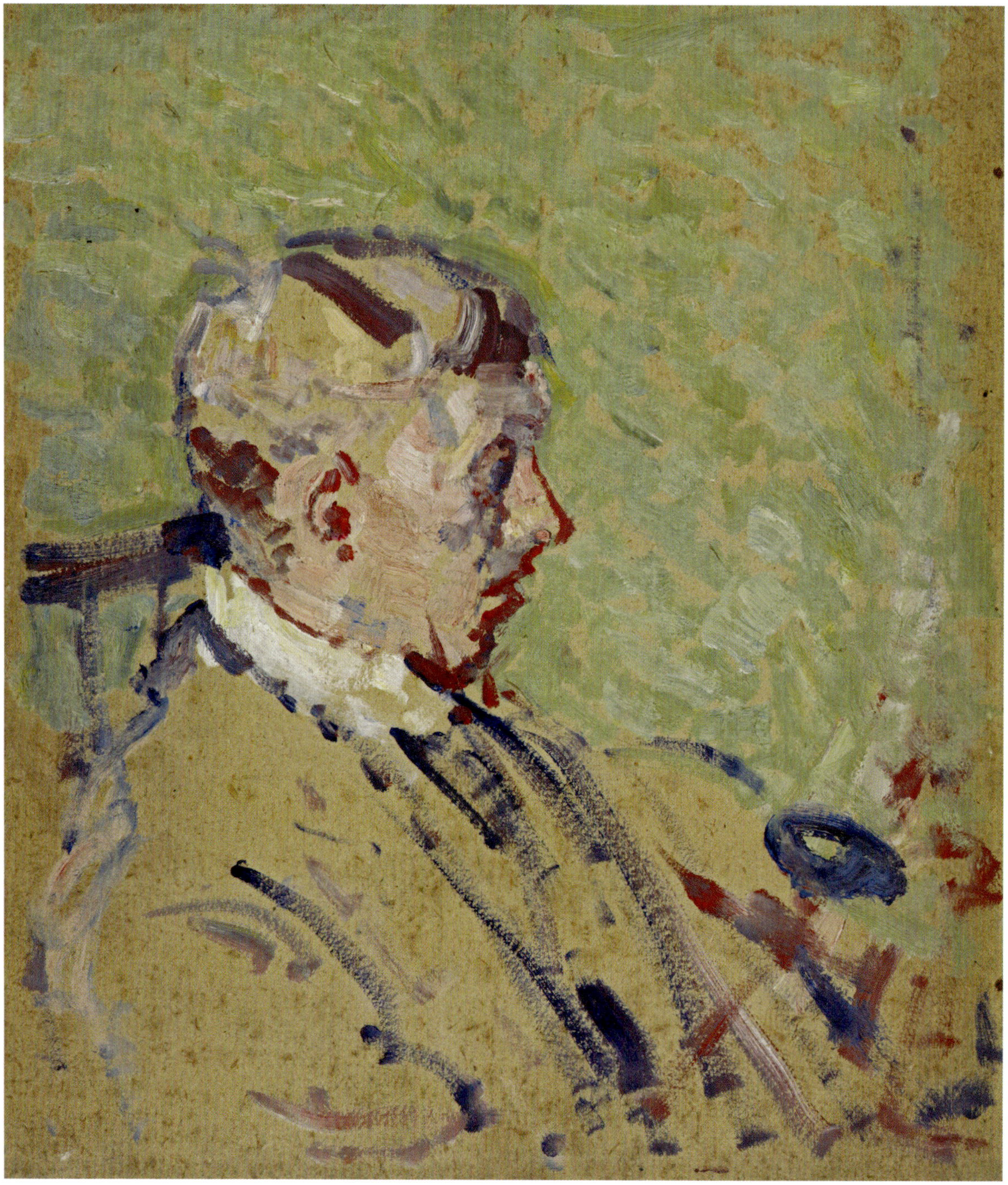

20 · Harold Gilman
Portrait of Spencer Gore, *c*.1911–12
Private collection

Bobby Bevan's father Robert was friends with the artists Harold Gilman and Spencer Gore and they worked together from 1908 until their respective deaths. The broadly sketched handling of this unfinished portrait of Gore by Gilman communicates the intimacy between the two painters.

21 · Harold Gilman *Madeleine Knox*, 1910–11
Private collection

Harold Gilman gave this meditative portrait to Robert Bevan, Bobby Bevan's father. Madeleine Knox (1890–1975) became a student of Walter Sickert's in 1908 and the following year they opened a school for etching in London. Knox later married Arthur Clifton of the Carfax Gallery, who was Sickert's dealer and who mounted the Camden Town Group exhibitions.

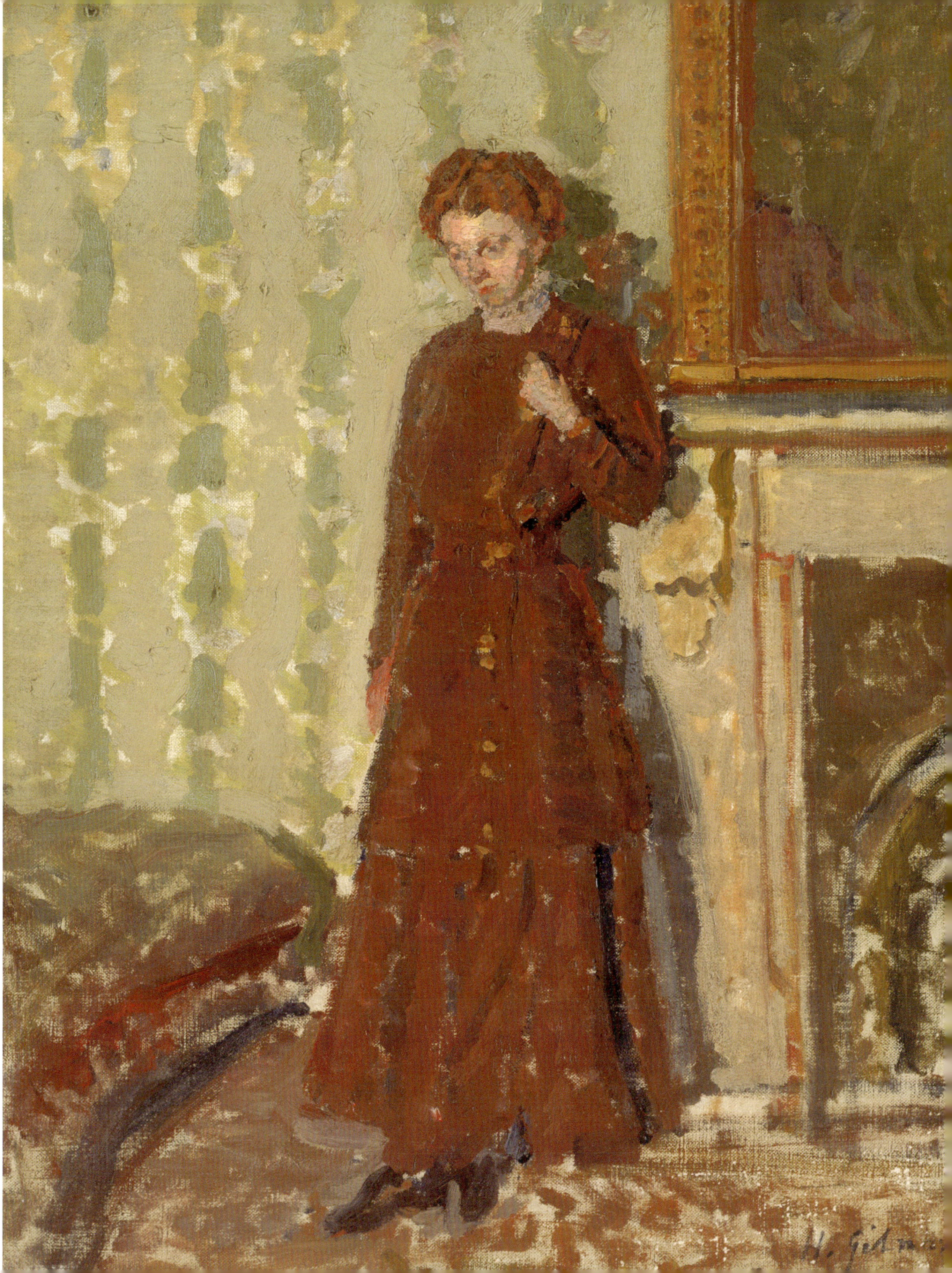

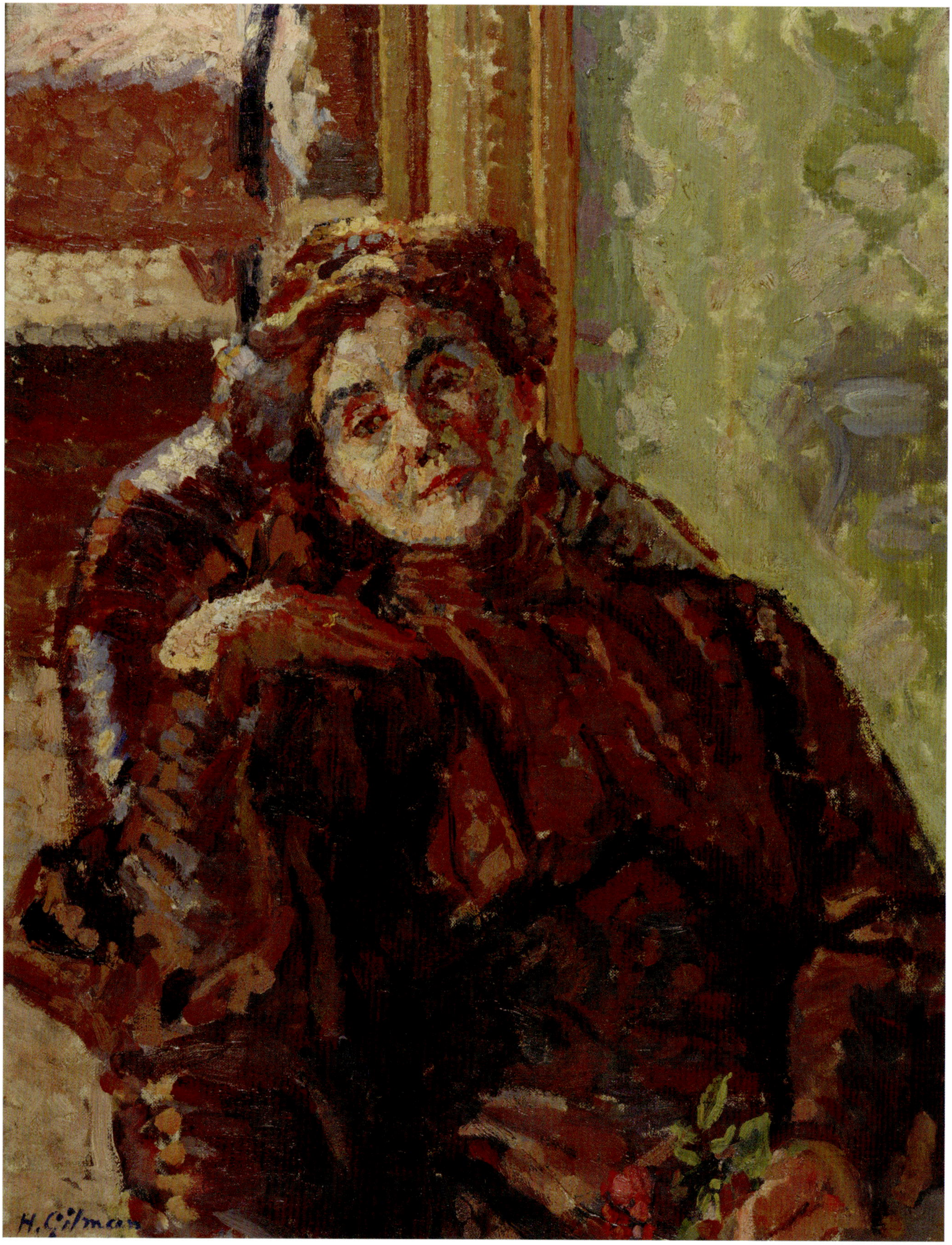
H. Gilman

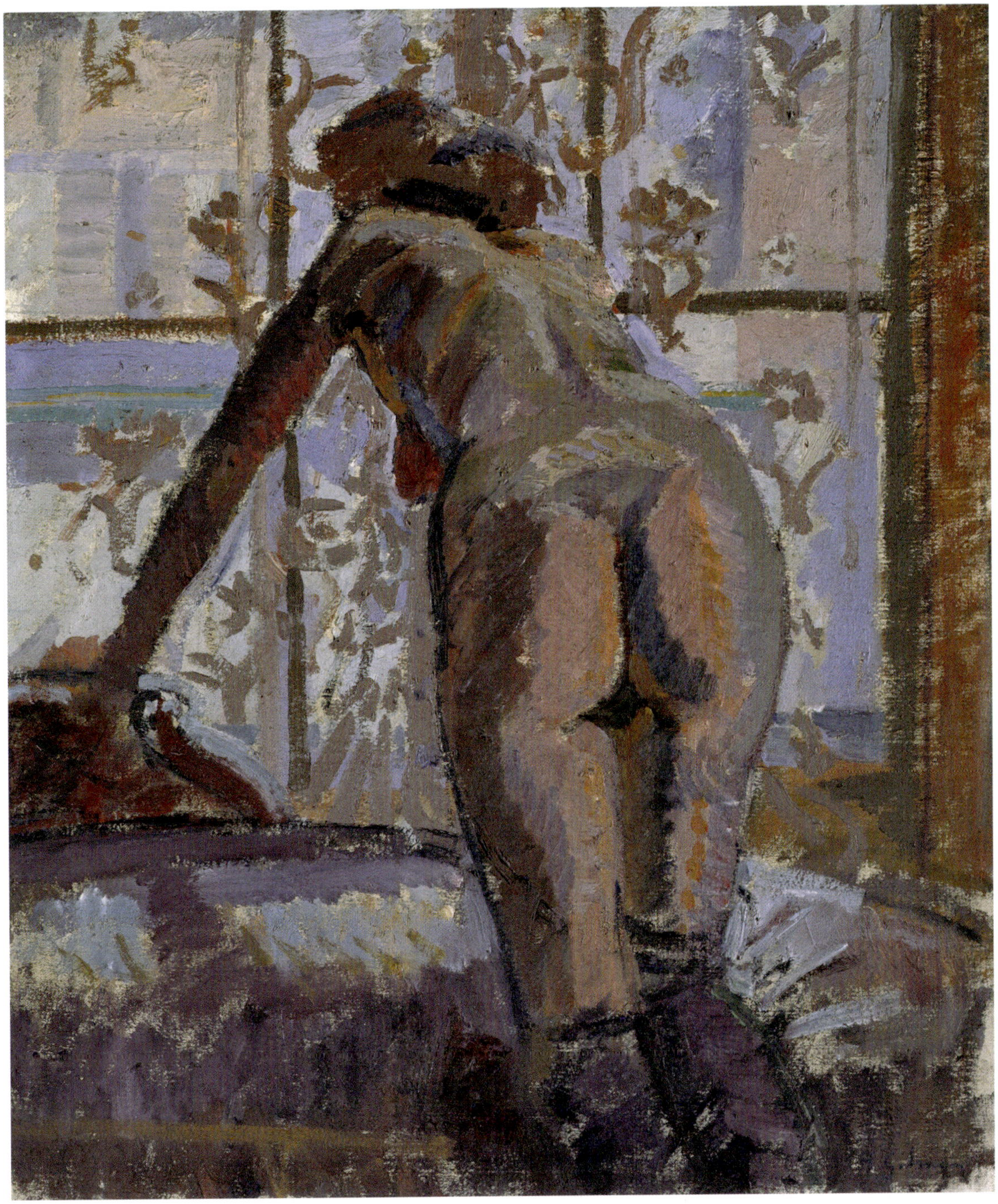

22 · Harold Gilman *Mrs Robert Bevan*, *c.*1913
Private collection

This is the second of three portraits which Harold Gilman painted of Bobby Bevan's mother, the artist Stanislawa de Karlowska. After Gilman's death, Bobby managed to buy all three, at different times, on the art market.

23 · Harold Gilman *Nude at a Window*, *c.*1912
Private collection

This picture belonged to Spencer Gore before it was acquired by Bobby Bevan's father, Robert. It is one of a series of nudes that Harold Gilman painted between 1911 and 1913, partly inspired by Walter Sickert's images of the same subject. *Nude at a Window* was hung in the library at Boxted House, visible only to those invited to enter Bobby's private study.

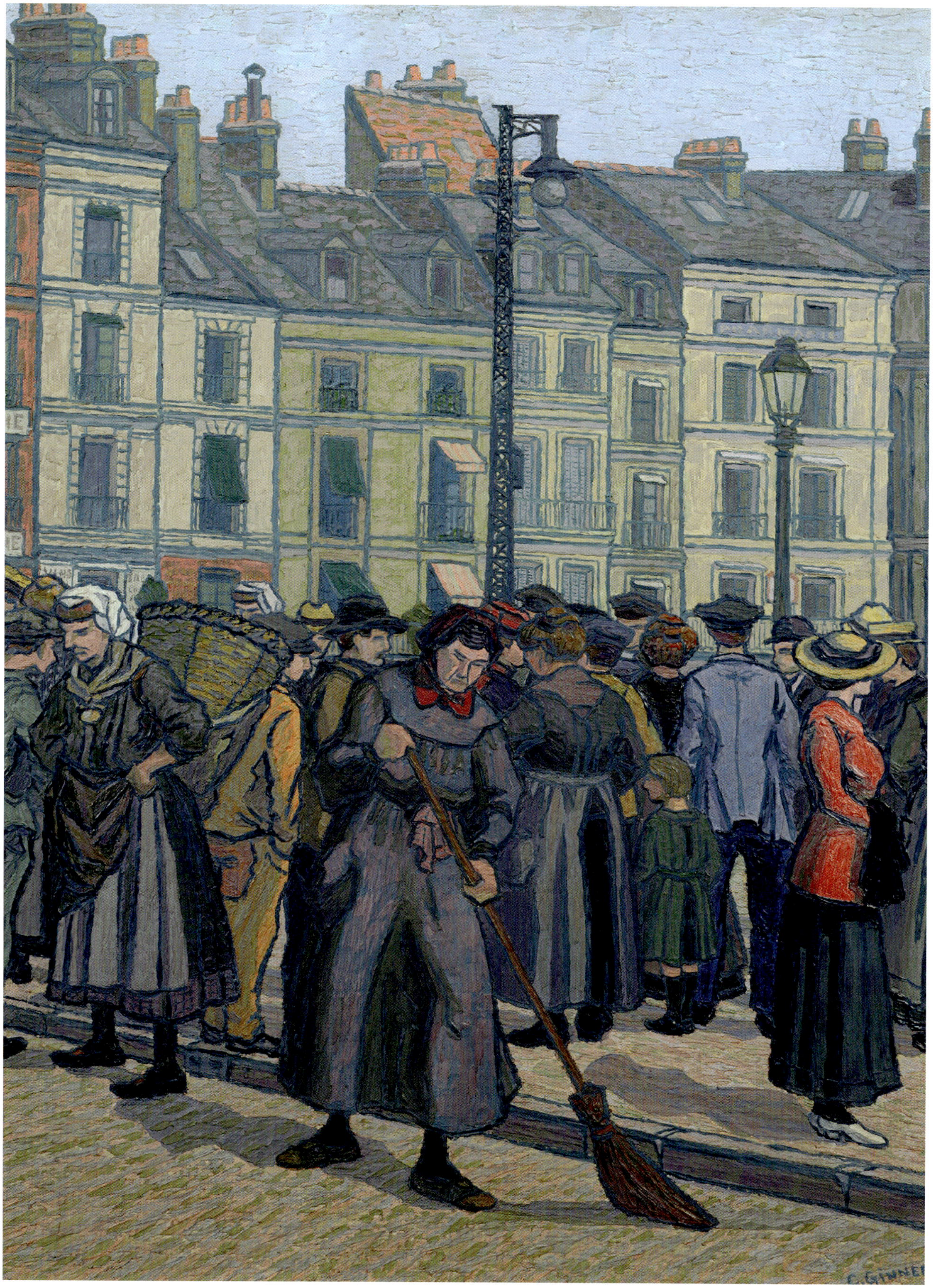

24 · Charles Ginner
La Vieille Balayeuse, Dieppe, 1913
Private collection

Charles Ginner was born in France and from 1910 was closely associated with Bobby Bevan's father, Robert Bevan, and other artists within his circle including Harold Gilman and Spencer Gore. Ginner exchanged this painting with Bevan for the latter's *The Town Field, Horsgate* of 1914, now in the collection of Reading Museum Service.

25 · Spencer Gore *Conversation Piece and Self-portrait*, c.1910
Private collection

Bobby Bevan's mother, the artist Stanislawa de Karlowska, bought this painting directly from Spencer Gore. It is an unusual self-portrait, as the artist appears only in reflection, partly obscured by a card stuck in the mirror's frame, whilst the focal point is the conversing china figures in the foreground, in an image composed of sophisticated spatial devices.

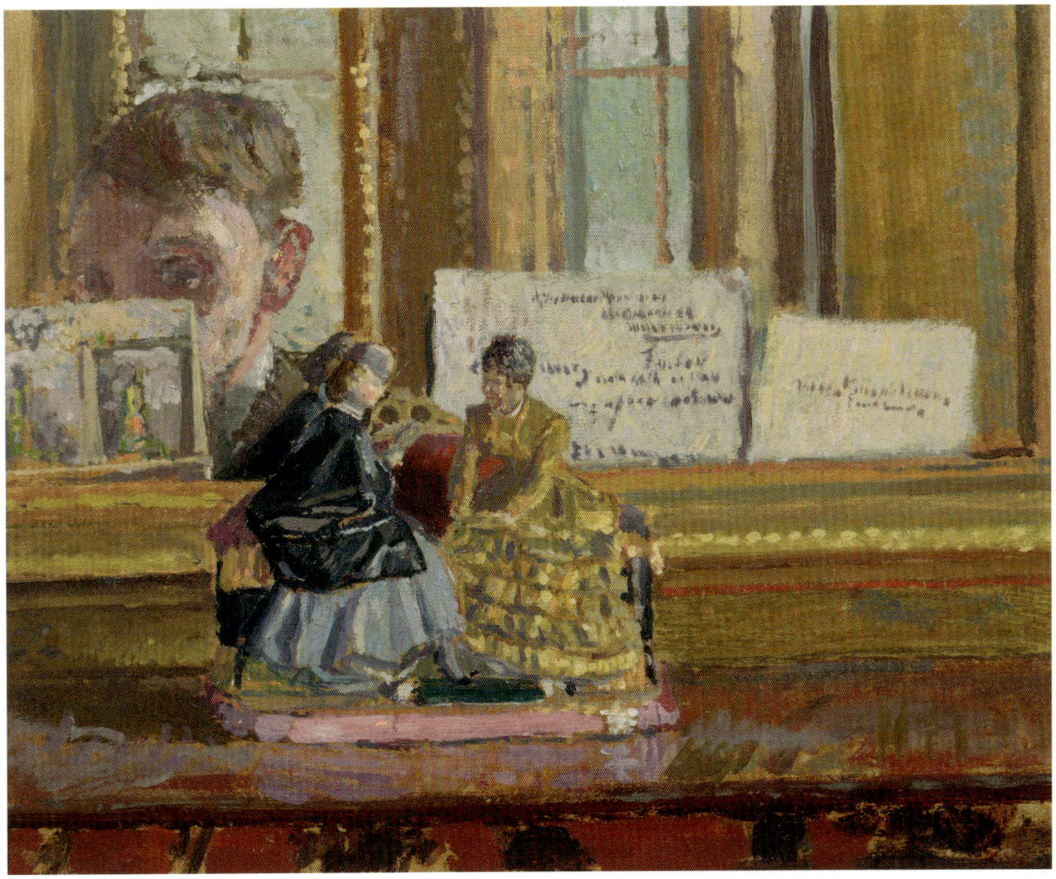

26 · Lett Haines *Piscatorial*, 1931
Private collection

Bobby and Natalie Bevan met Lett Haines and his partner Cedric Morris in London in the 1920s. Their friendship blossomed after the Bevans married and moved to Boxted House in 1947, about twelve miles from Haines's and Morris's Benton End home and art school near Hadleigh. Haines worked primarily on paper, as is the case with *Piscatorial*, which is a decorative example of his figurative work of the 1930s.

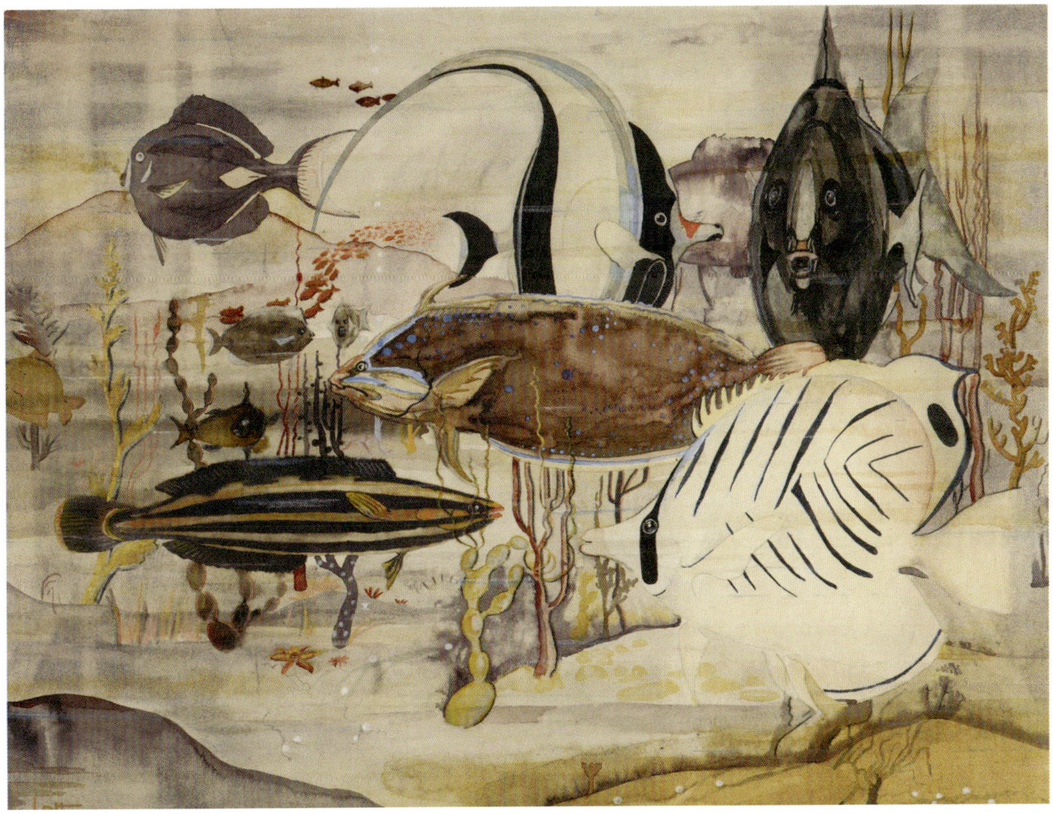

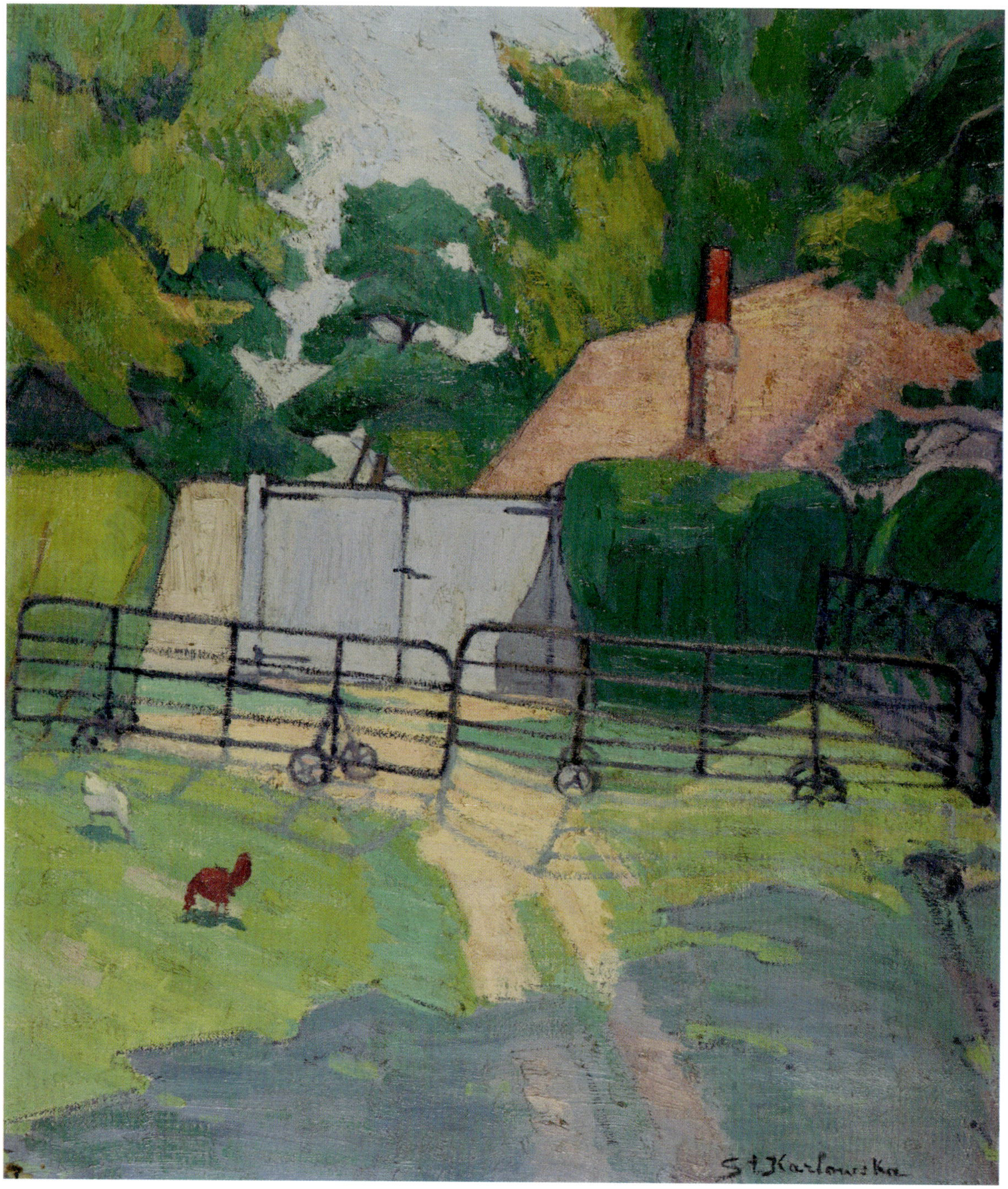

27 · Stanislawa de Karlowska
The Stable Field, Horsgate, *c.*1914
Private collection

Bobby Bevan's mother, Stanislawa de Karlowska, studied at the Académie Julian in Paris, and continued to paint after the birth of her children, Edith in 1898 and Bobby in 1901. This work depicts part of the Horsgate estate, Robert Bevan's childhood home in Cuckfield, West Sussex.

28 · Stanislawa de Karlowska
Backs of Houses, Percy Street, *c.*1919
Private collection

A founding member of the London Group with Robert Bevan, Karlowska painted a number of works depicting the urban landscape of London. In 1935 the artist and Tate Gallery director J.B. Manson wrote of her work: 'She finds beauty in the most ordinary scenes: street corners, the backs of houses and so on and with such "motifs" she produces satisfying works of art.'

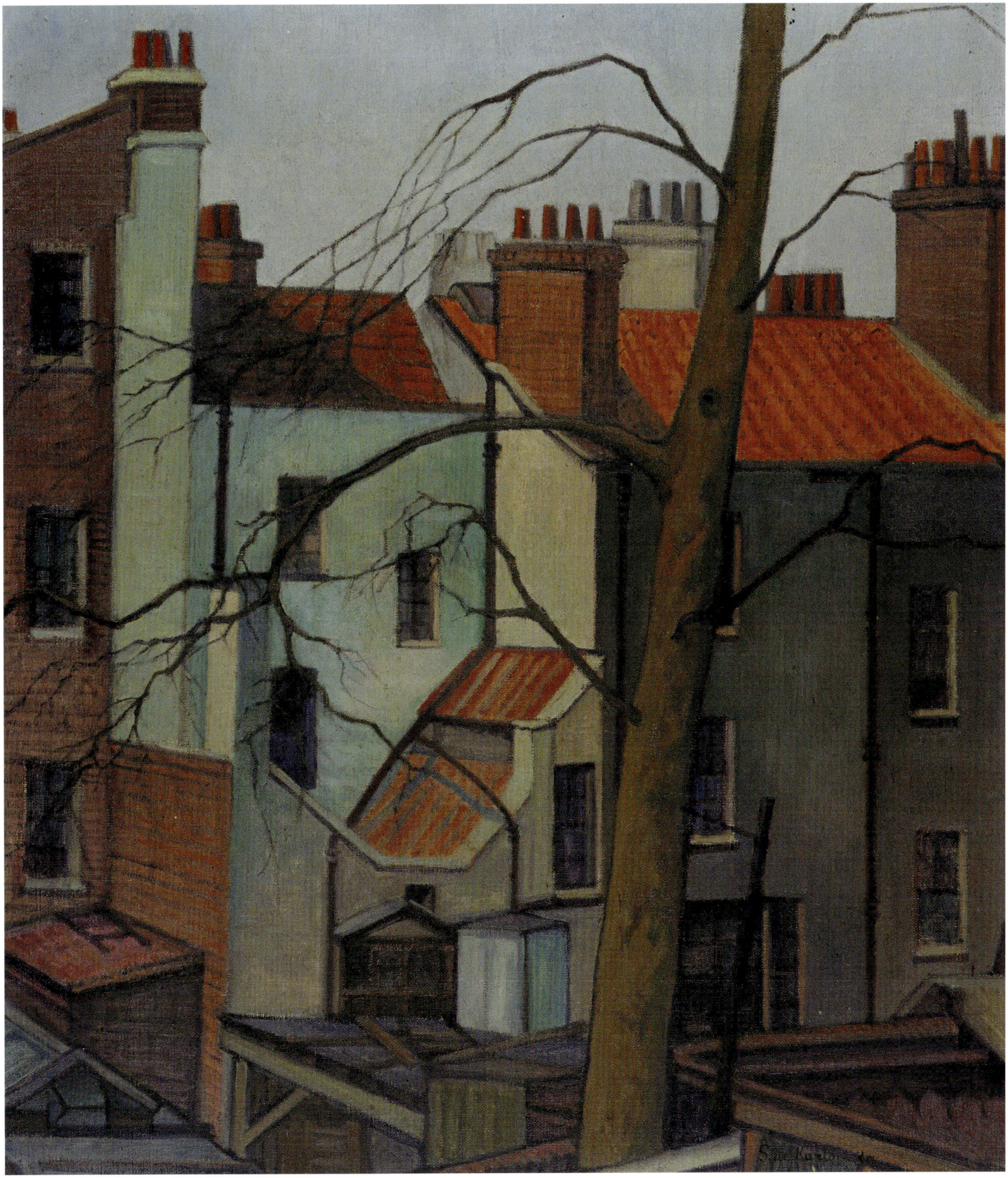

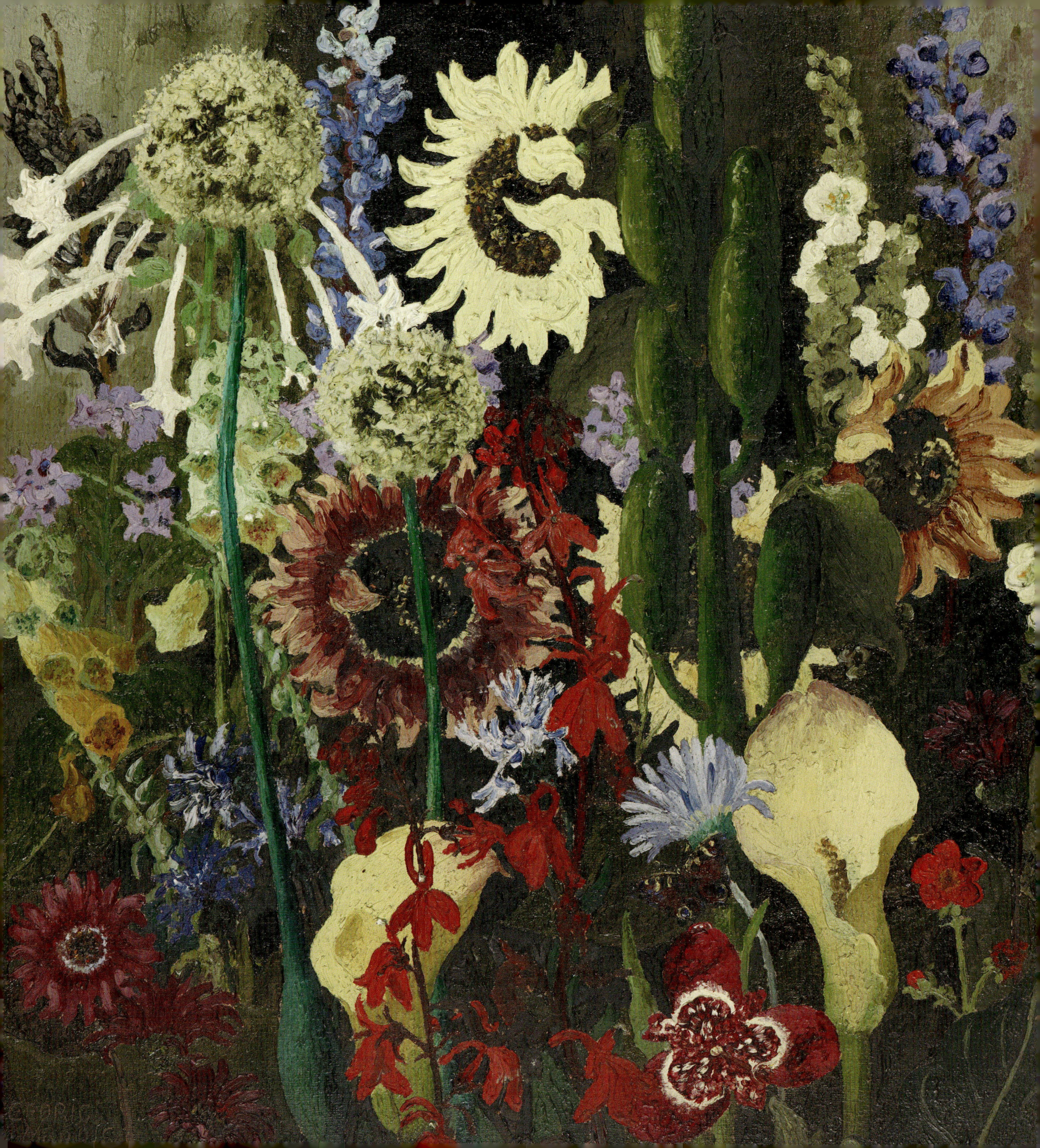

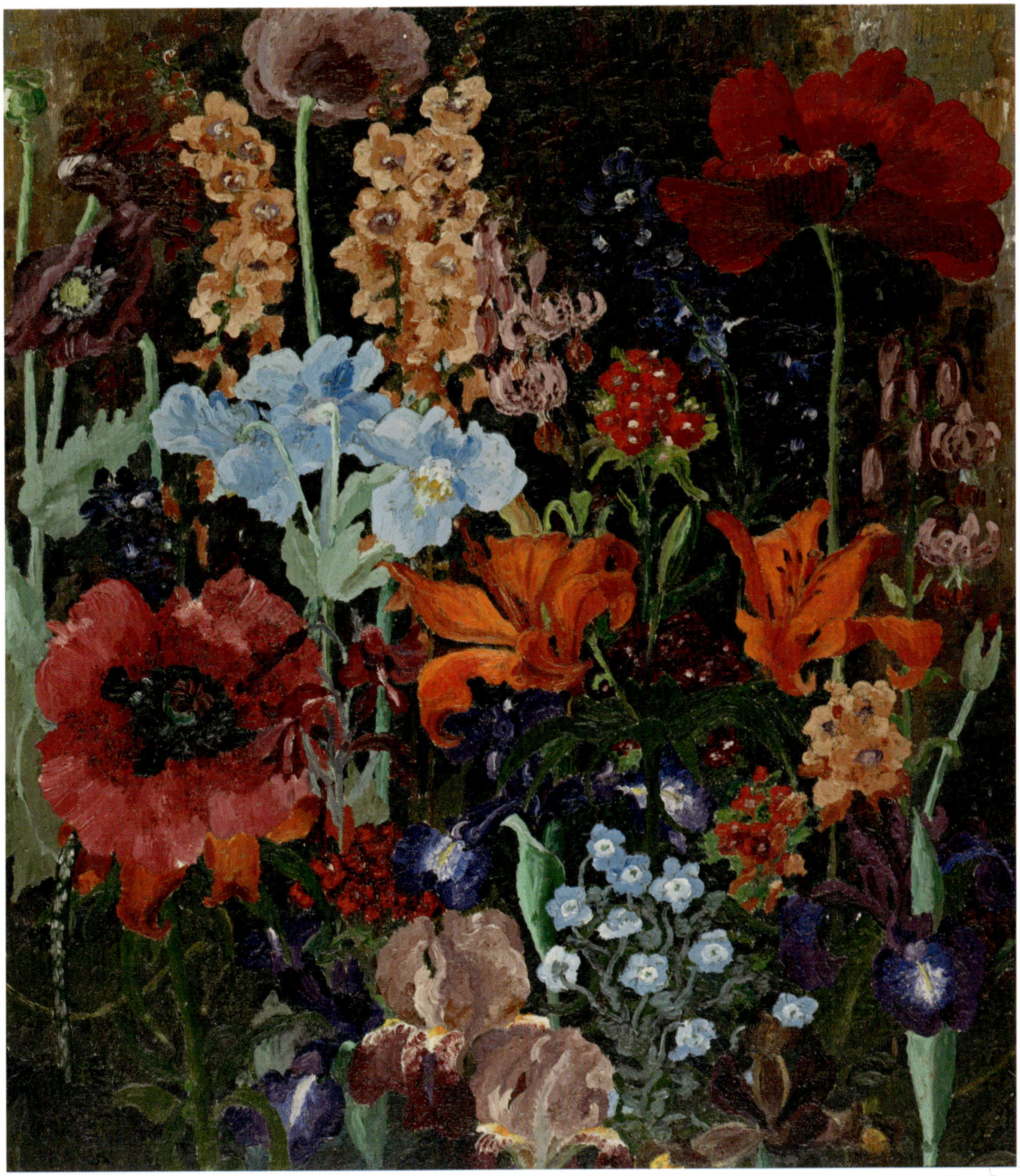

29 · Cedric Morris *Paysage du Jardin no.2*, 1931
Private collection

Bobby Bevan was part of the social set who met at Cedric Morris and, his partner, Lett Haines's house, The Pound, in Higham, Suffolk throughout the 1930s. Bobby probably acquired *Paysage du Jardin no.2* during that period. Morris was as much a plantsman as an artist and this work exemplifies his botanical interest and preferred subject matter, uncompromising compositions, use of strong colours and feel for the texture of paint itself.

30 · Cedric Morris *The Blue Poppy*, 1932
Private collection

Cedric Morris was a celebrated plantsman and the subjects of *The Blue Poppy* are most likely to be flowers which he grew in his renowned garden at his home, The Pound, in Higham. Indeed, he later bred an oriental poppy, known as *Papaver orientale* 'Cedric Morris', with ashen-pink petals which spread out from a purple-black centre.

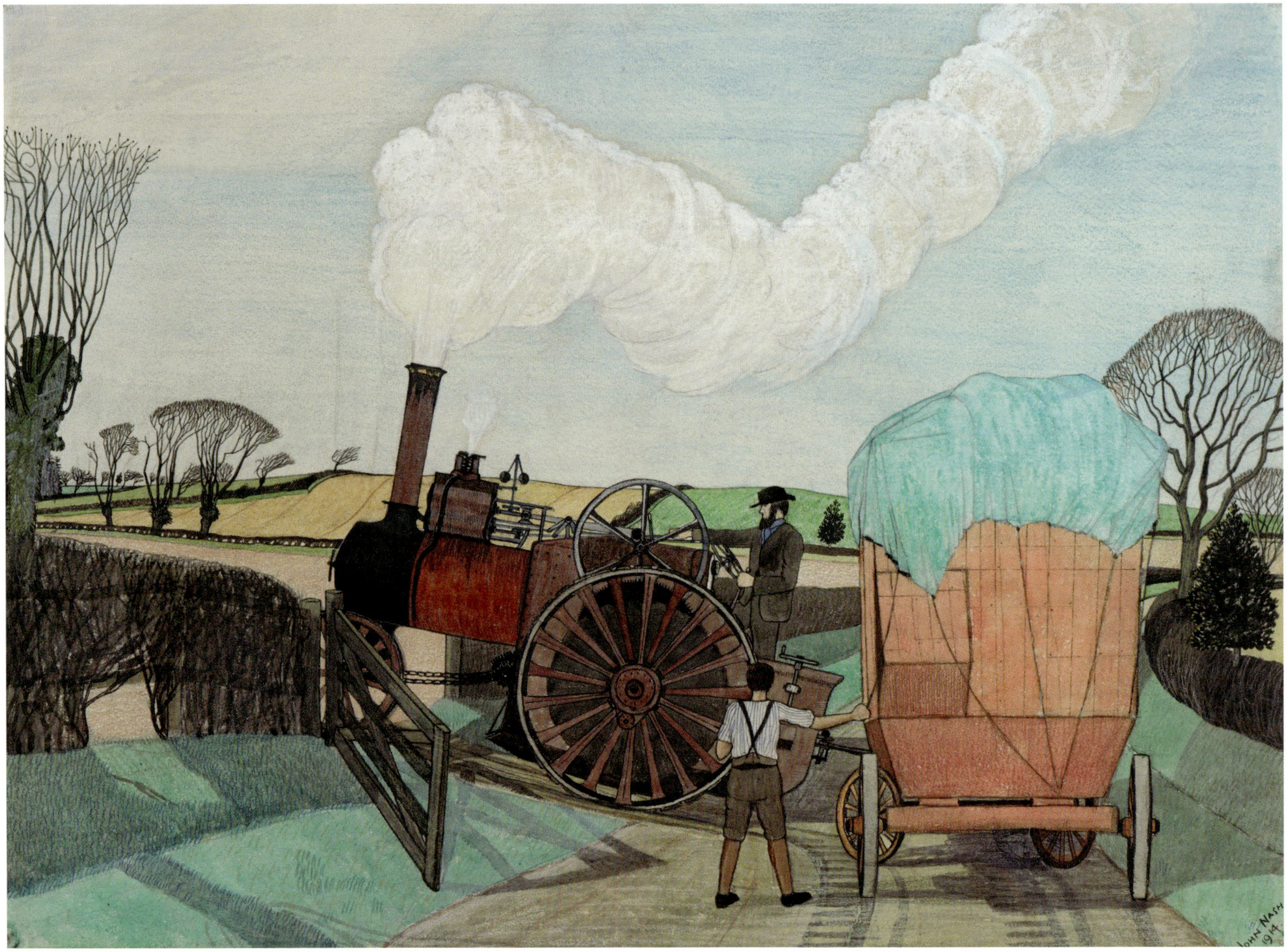

31 · John Nash *The Threshing Machine*, 1914
Private collection

John Nash was an intimate of the Boxted House circle: Bobby Bevan knew Nash from childhood as he exhibited with his father Robert Bevan in 1913. Natalie Bevan met him in the late 1920s and Nash illustrated books by her first husband, Lance Sieveking. Nash and his wife, Christine, moved to Wormingford in 1945, six miles from Boxted House and they were very close to the Bevans for the rest of their lives. Nash created this watercolour whilst working with his brother, the artist, Paul Nash, as agricultural labourers, harvesting in Dorset.

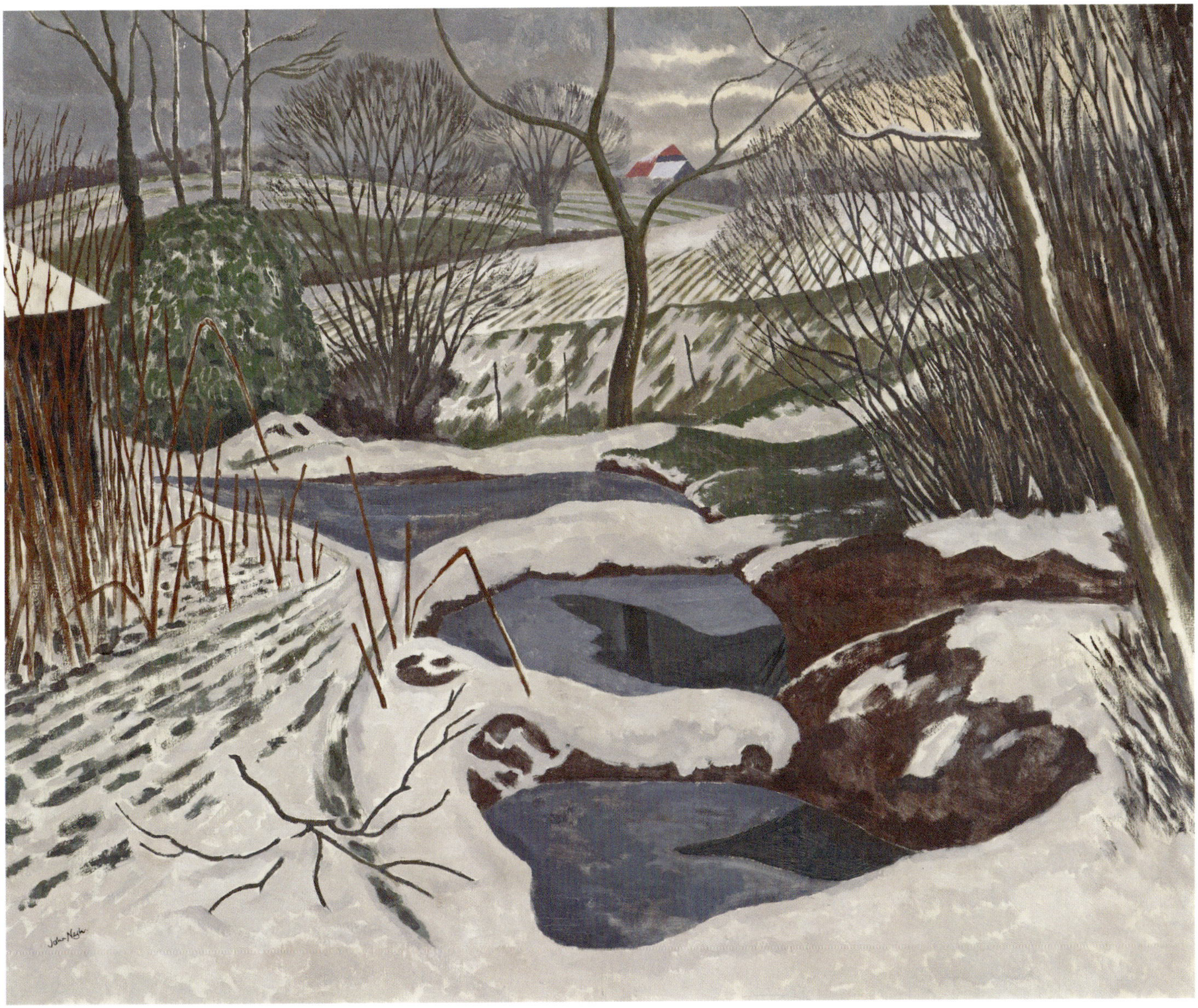

32 · John Nash *Ice and Snow*, 1959
Private collection

Ice and Snow depicts part of the garden at John Nash's Essex home, Bottengoms, in Wormingford not far from Boxted House. Nash was particularly interested in painting snowscapes, especially the contrast between the pure white of the snow and the brown-green vegetable life which emerged through it.

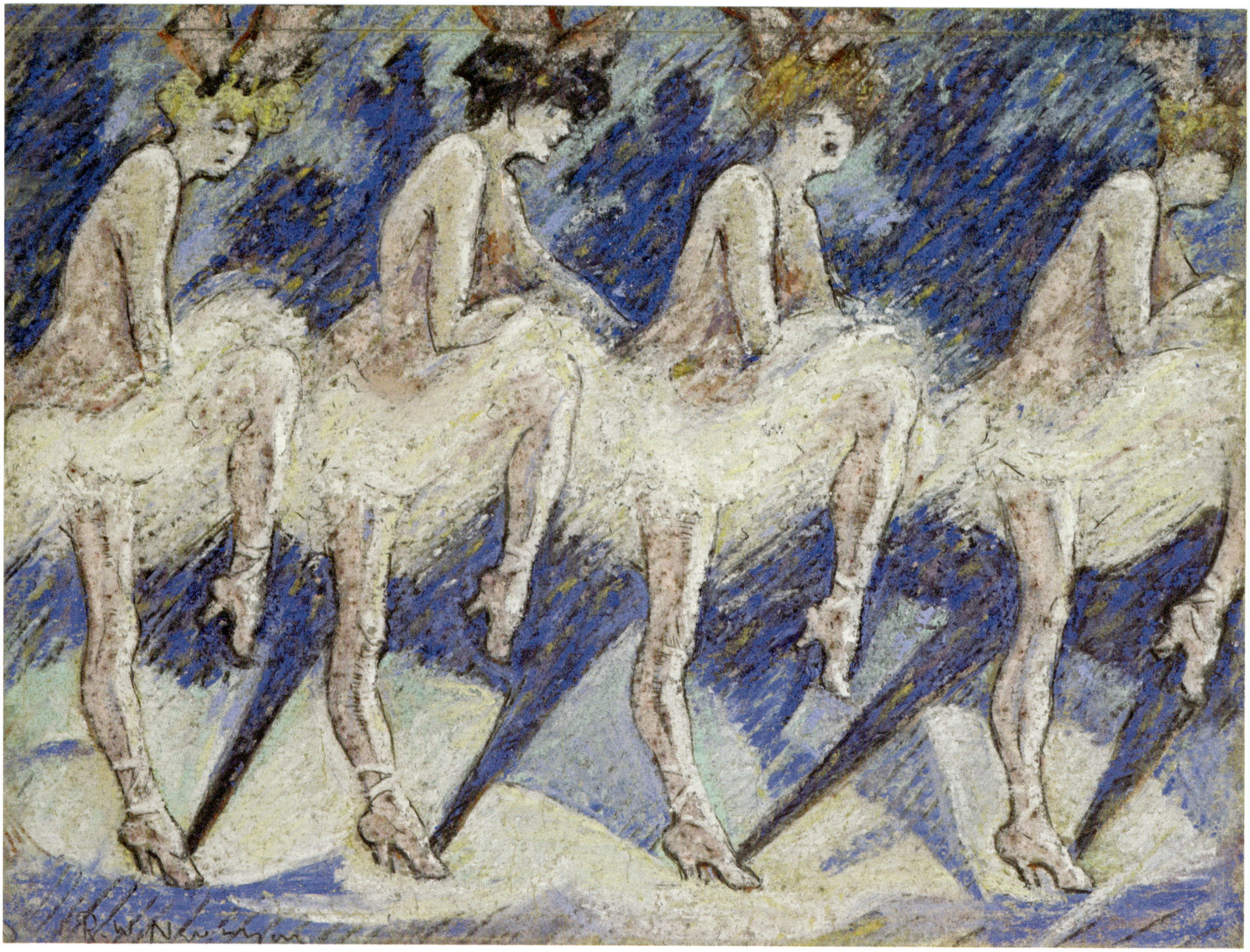

33 · Christopher R.W. Nevinson *Broadway Girls*, *c.*1919
Private collection

Natalie Bevan met Christopher Nevinson in London in 1927. The following year, aged eighteen, she travelled to Paris with Nevinson, his wife, Kathleen and the artist Harry Jonas on a working holiday. Nevinson drew *Broadway Girls* during his stay in New York in May 1919. He found the modern, dynamic city fascinating and a great source of inspiration. Natalie's family felt this image summed up her own joie de vivre.

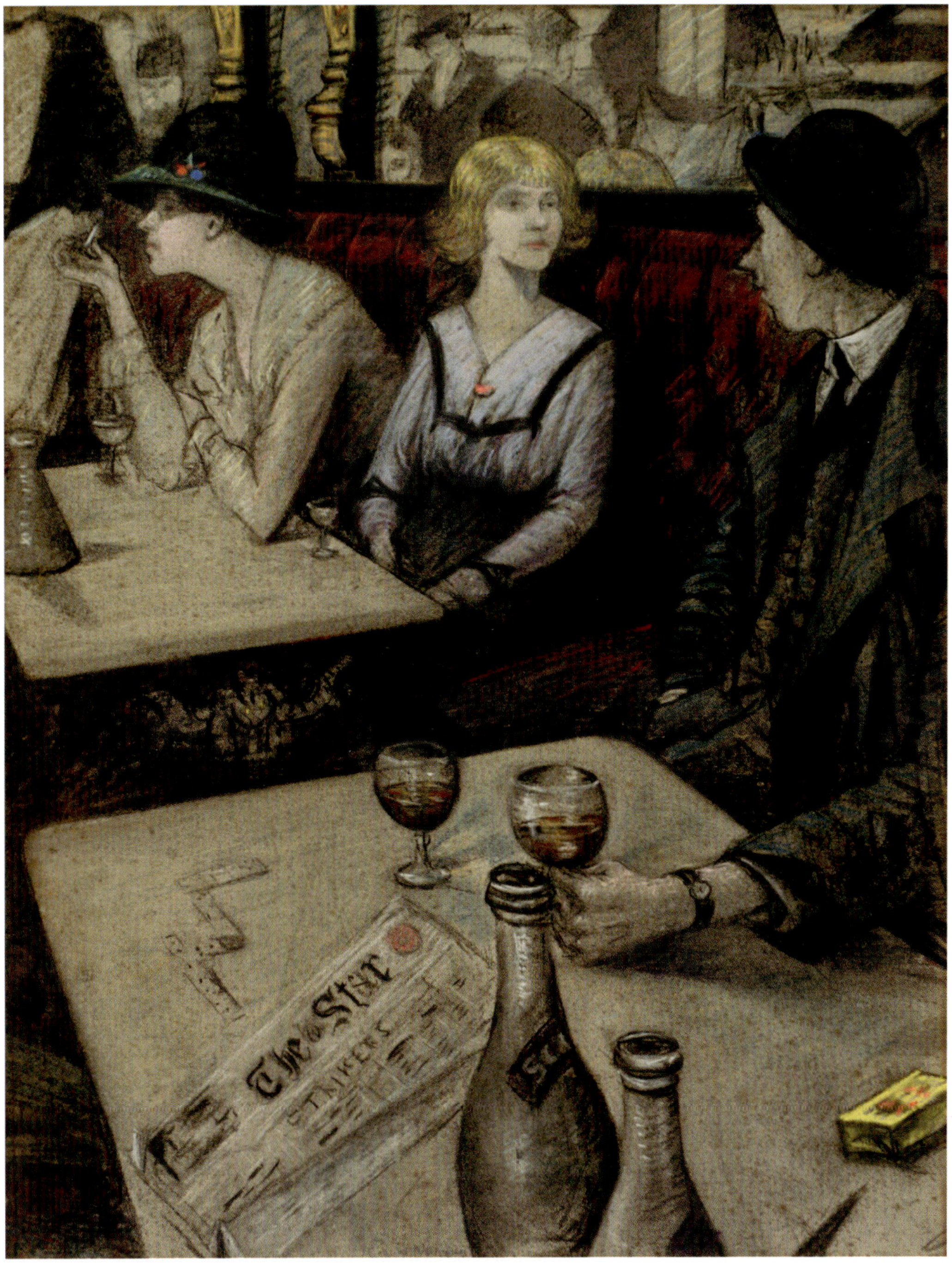

34 · Christopher R.W. Nevinson
The Lilies of the Café, *c*.1919
Private collection

This work was included in Christopher Nevinson's *Peace* exhibition at the Leicester Galleries, London in 1919. In its depiction of the mundanity beneath the surface of an apparently glamorous social situation, it recalls the work of the French nineteenth-century painter, Edgar Degas and in particular his painting *L'Absinthe* of 1875–6, now in the Musée d'Orsay, Paris.

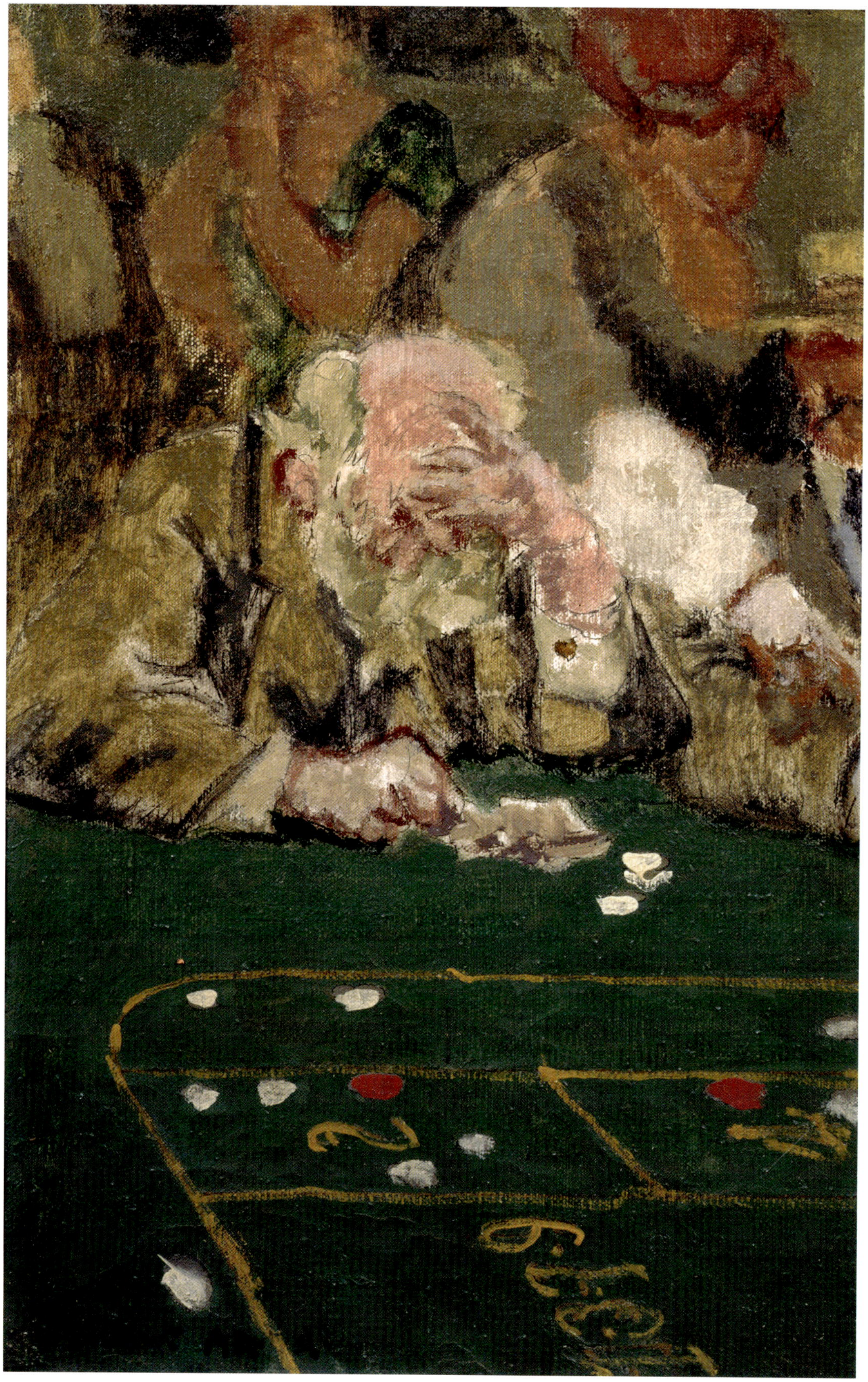

35 · Walter Sickert
The System, 1924–8
Private collection

Walter Sickert was a leading figure in the London art world of the early twentieth century and was a friend and colleague of Bobby Bevan's father, Robert Bevan. *The System* comes from a series of paintings based on drawings Sickert made in the casino at Dieppe, which was the centre of fashionable life in the popular French resort. Natalie hung this painting in her sitting-room at Boxted House.

36 · Henri de Toulouse-Lautrec
Divan Japonais, 1892–3
Private collection

As a leading figure in the advertising world, Bobby Bevan had a professional interest in the promotional work of Toulouse-Lautrec, as well as a personal interest in his art as exceptional works on paper. This lithograph was produced as a poster for the Parisian café-concert, the Divan Japonais, in January 1893. It features the dancer Jane Avril with the writer and critic Edouard Dujardin in the foreground and the singer Yvette Guilbert on the stage, recognisable only by her black gloves.

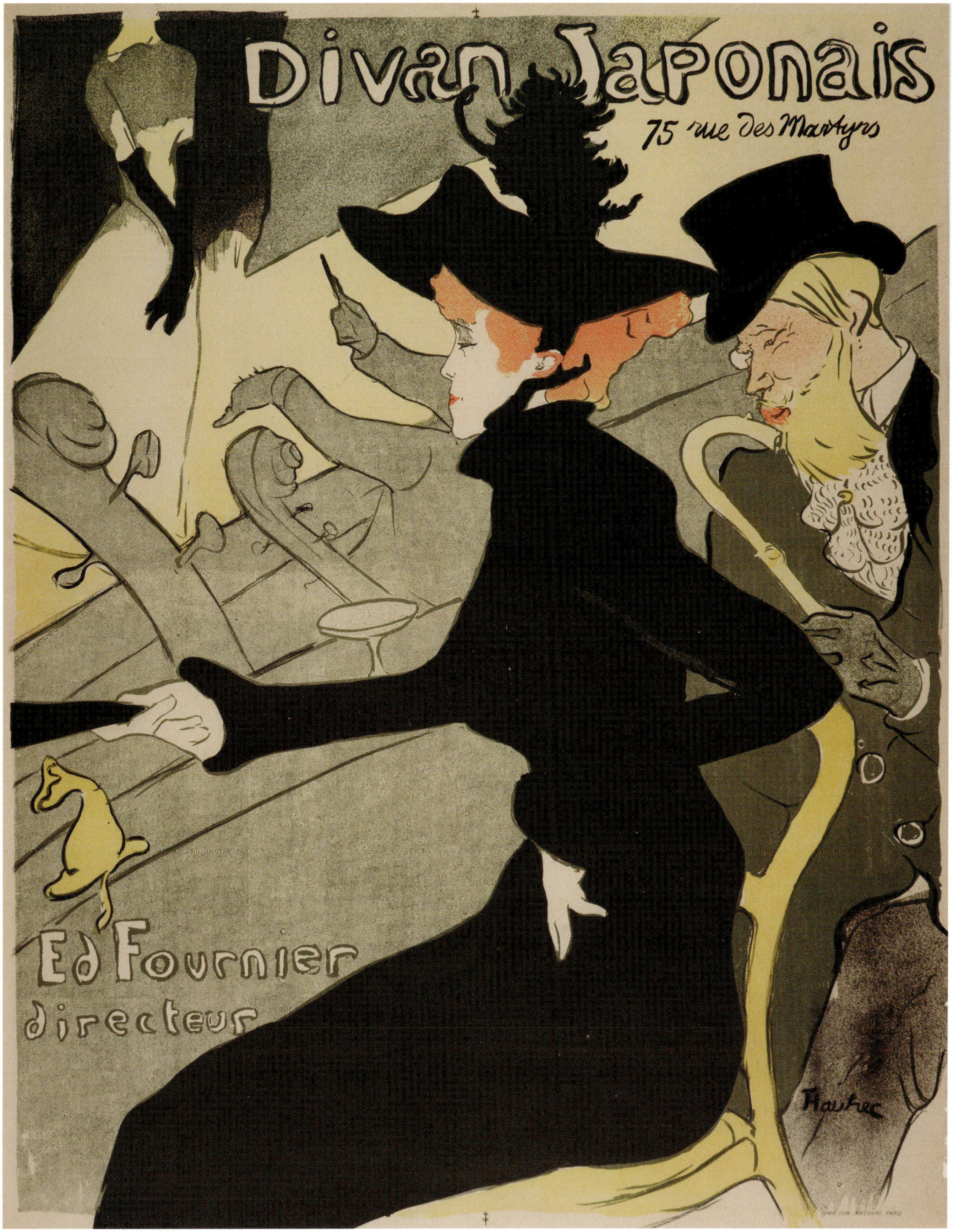
Divan Japonais
75 rue des Martyrs
Ed Fournier
directeur

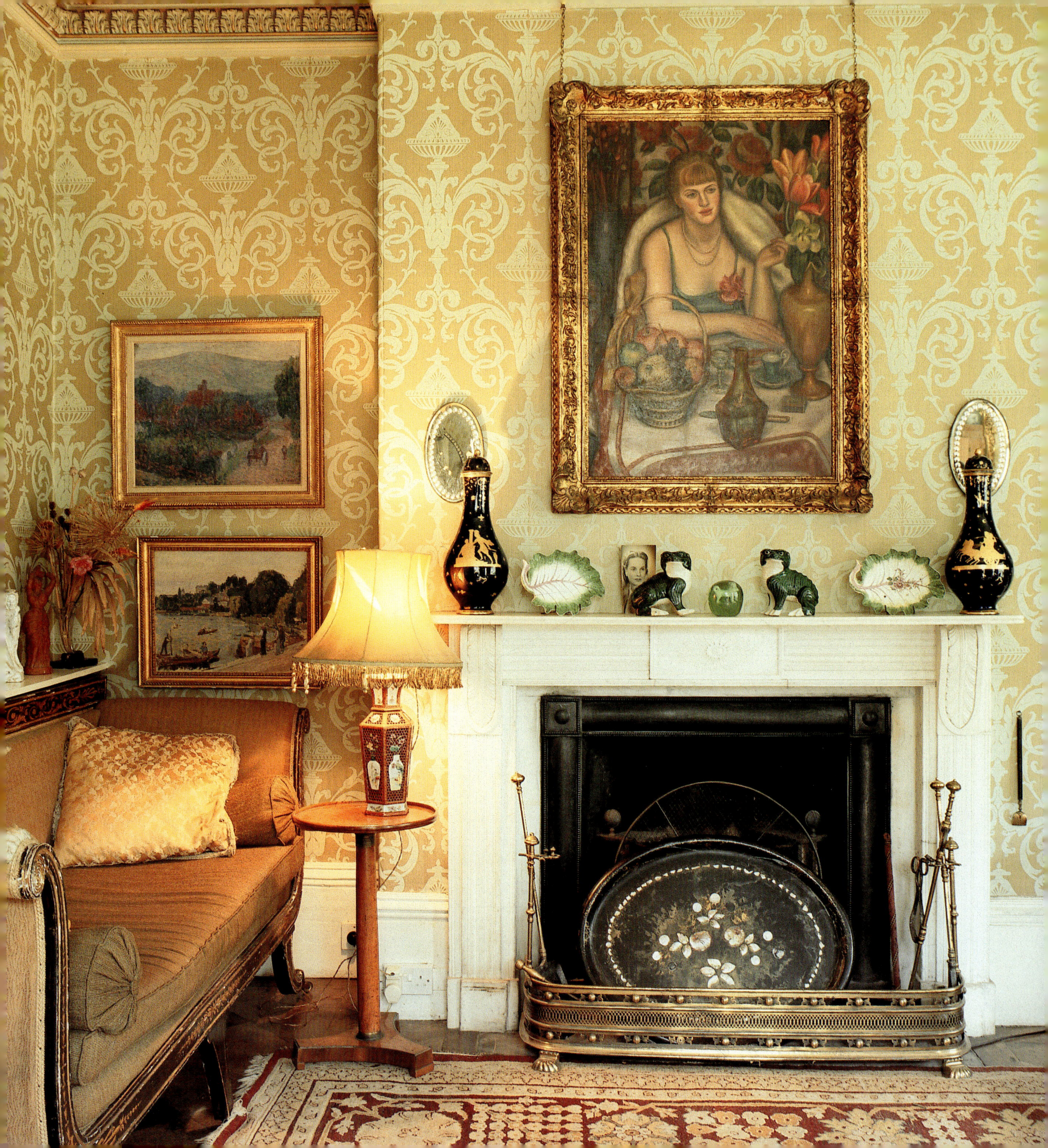

Memories of Natalie Bevan at Boxted

CAROLINE CUTHBERT

Fig. 26 · The drawing-room at Boxted House with *Supper (Natalie Denny)* by Mark Gertler above the fireplace.

IN December 1965 Bobby Bevan was surprised to read a review by John Russell in *The Sunday Times* of an exhibition of sixty drawings and pastels by Claude-Emile Schuffenecker being shown in a gallery he had never heard of. The artist had a special resonance for Bobby: his father, Robert Polhill Bevan, when he was living at the Villa Julia in Pont-Aven in the early 1890s, had painted with Schuffenecker. The gallery turned out to be some small rooms upstairs in Vigo Street, close by the back entrance of Albany, and the rather unlikely show had been put together by a man in his twenties called Anthony d'Offay.

Bobby was immediately taken both by Anthony's knowledge and the quality of the work in the gallery; and this first affinity developed into a hugely enjoyable friendship between the two men over the next nine years until Bobby's death in December 1974. Central to it was their intense interest not only in the Camden Town Group but in the whole of twentieth-century British art and its influences. They would view sales, discuss prices and buy pictures; and then re-hang the collection at Boxted together to show off the new acquisitions. These re-hanging visits to Boxted were a special treat for Anthony, who was equally won over by Bobby's wife Natalie.

I joined the gallery in April 1973 (coinciding with the introduction of VAT on the sale of works of art). I remember the stir of anticipation before a visit from Bobby and Natalie. They were a strikingly glamorous couple, Bobby tall and rather imposing in expensive well-cut suits, and Natalie, immaculately made-up, golden hair in an elegant chignon, very soignée with beautiful clothes and jewellery[fig.27]. In London she often wore a striped high-necked silk shirt with a skirt under a matching long jacket or coat, probably of thick Indian silk, never without a dashing hat with a brim, rather like a bowler, and into the band at the front would be tucked several real flowers – maybe mixed pink and red geraniums – or a bunch of spotted guinea-fowl feathers. After Bobby's death she would often come to Dering Street and Anthony would take her out to special openings and the best restaurants that she was used to going to with Bobby. She was very friendly to me and before long I was invited to Boxted about which I had heard so much.

Arriving there by car, one scrunched round the sweep of the drive, past the

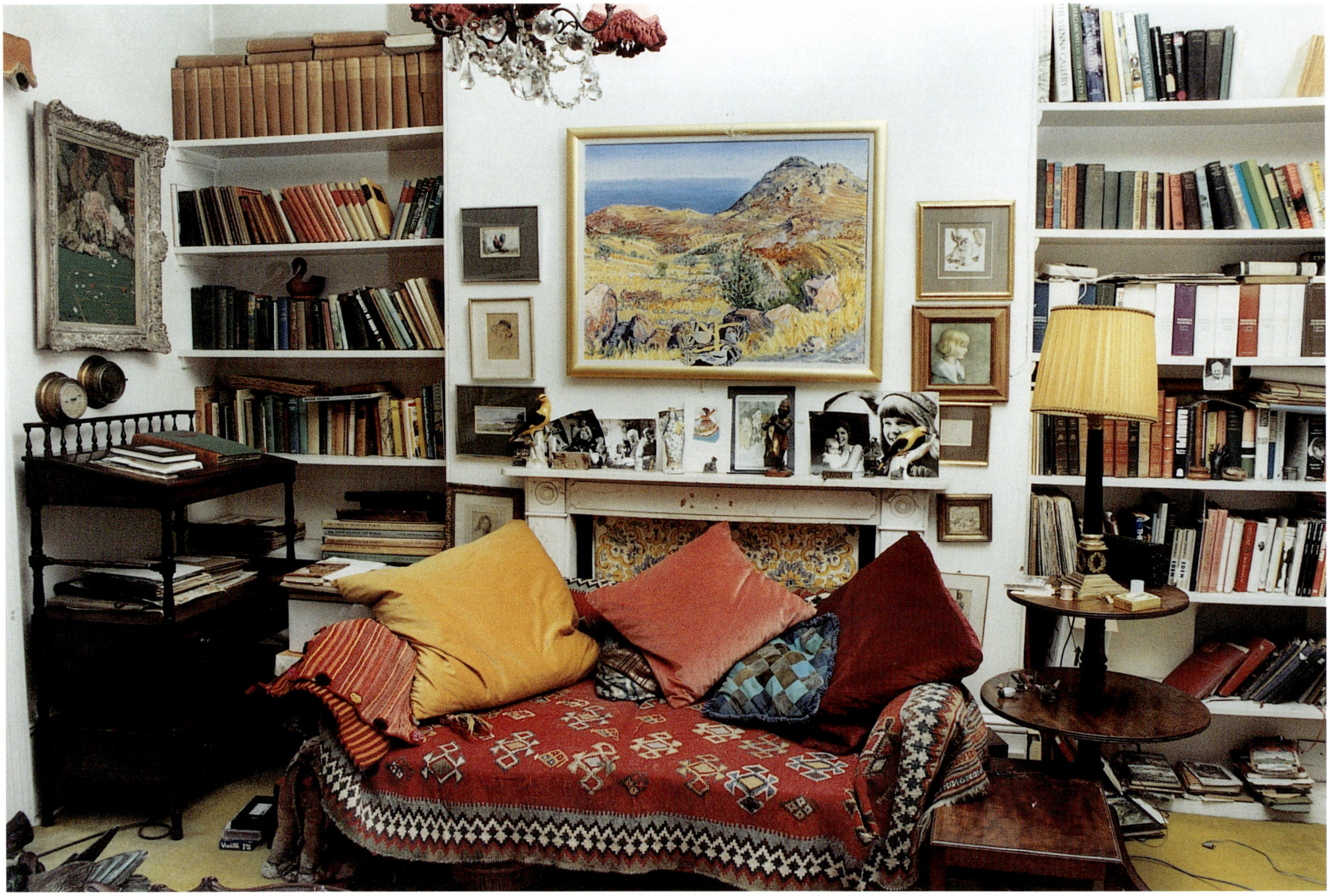

Fig. 27 · Natalie's sitting-room in Boxted House with works by Frederick Gore and Walter Sickert on the walls. A portrait of Natalie in profile as a child by her mother, Alice Denny, is on the wall to the right of the mantelpiece.

Fig. 28 · Natalie Bevan, 1947
Private collection

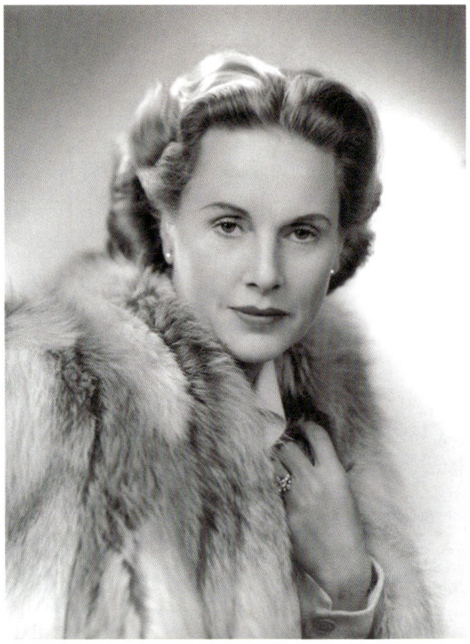

high-walled vegetable garden and up to the pillared entrance, to be greeted on the doorstep by Natalie with a cheerful, laughing: 'Hello-lo-lo'. The hall was lit from a sunny room on the left, Natalie's sitting-room: a bright yellow carpet, a red kilim, patterned cushions and more kilims scattered over chairs and sofas, Robert Bevan's blaze of colour *Evening in the Culme Valley* and the enchanting little *Gate at Szeliwy* either side of her writing table, Sickert's *The System* hanging beside the door open to the conservatory, a dense jungle with a Japanese kite peeping out [fig.27].

On the right of the hall was the greeny-gold drawing-room, an Aladdin's cave of wonderful things: Mark Gertler's 'Supper',

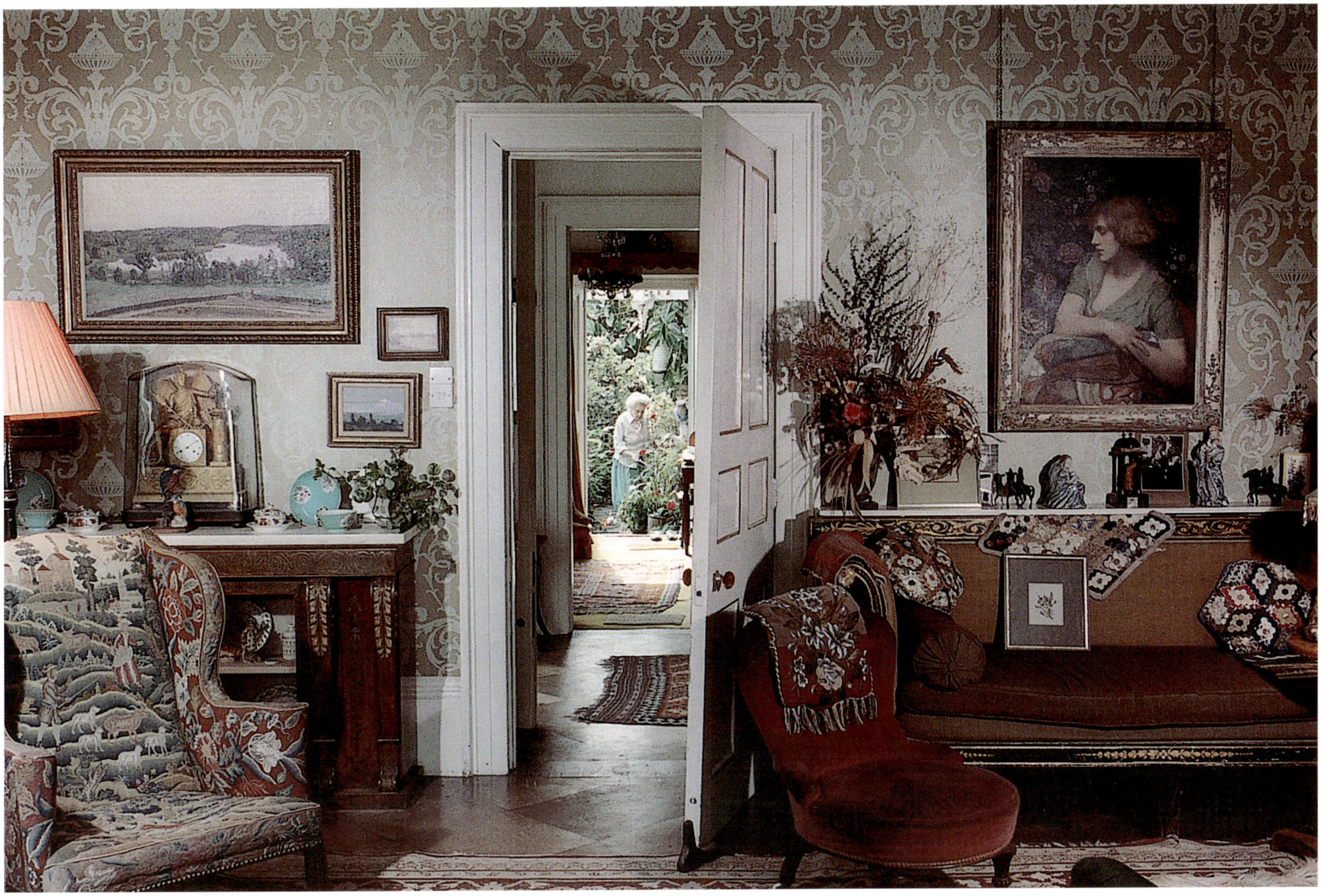

the arresting portrait of the beautiful young Natalie Denny, over the fireplace, eighteenth-century furniture, a grand French pier glass and an oval Regency Irish mirror with glittering glass buttons bought in Dublin in 1922 between the windows; then Chelsea dessert plates of green cabbage leaves with pink and orange fruit, more Bevan paintings, Gilman's 'Swedish Landscape', a little Gore 'Boating at Richmond', one of Cedric Morris's flower pieces and a surprising nude by Sir William Etty. The French windows looked over a small pond with a half-sunken rowing boat, down the lawn, past shrubs with lurking statues and beyond the ha-ha to the fields painted by John Nash [fig.29].

The hall itself was hung with drawings and paintings, Henry Lamb and John Armstrong, above a Regency bookcase covered with china and painted stones from Aldeburgh, the creaky parquet floor in an unusual diamond pattern designed by Natalie. A curved wall at the end of the hall led via a passage to the library hung with 'La Vieille Balayeuse' by Charles Ginner, Gilman's portraits of Mrs Robert Bevan, the standing figure of Madeleine Knox and his saucy *Nude at a Window*, and Spencer Gore's 'Conversation Piece' a self-portrait just visible as a reflection in a mirror half obscured by cards. One wall was almost taken up by an impressive break-front bookcase, another with more books on

Fig. 29 · Looking from the drawing-room, through Natalie's sitting-room, to the studio-conservatory at Boxted House. Works by Harold Gilman, Thomas Churchyard, Robert Bevan and a portrait of Natalie by George Spencer Watson are on the walls.

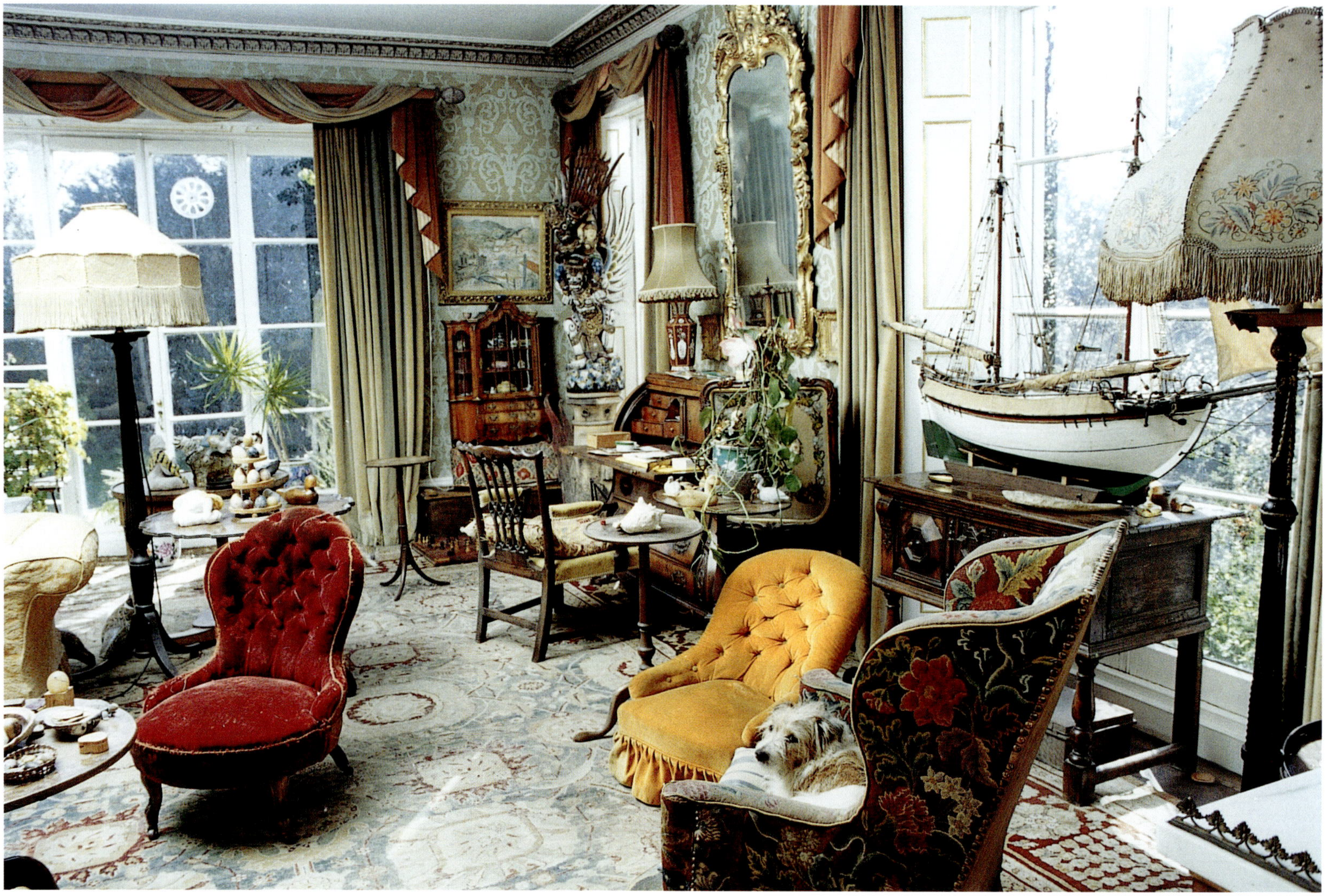

Fig. 30 · The drawing-room at Boxted House, with Harry the dog and a painting by Natalie hanging in the corner.

shelves, while Bobby's desk stood in the window looking out over the garden.

Down the passage was a gallery of drawings, double-hung – lots of Bevans, a Gilman or two and several Gaudier-Brzeskas – and leading to the glowing ruby red dining-room. Here one was immediately struck by the imposing portrait by Gertler of his mother, hanging pendant to Bevan's 'Gravelye Farm', and, opposite, several paintings by Bevan over a Regency sideboard cabinet displaying an orange and gold Derby dinner service. The unusual *The Green Coat* by Bevan – of his wife's green velvet coat lying on a chair, her black hat with feathers propped on the back – hung to the left of more French windows. These opened to an outside dining-table under a pergola covered with vines, where a flock of guinea-fowl tip-toed about scratching for crumbs.

Next came the pantry-cum-flower-room, where champagne corks popped before lunch in a general stream of 'little drinks', then a back hall to the bright yellow kitchen, the joins between the old grey flag-stones picked out in white. The wooden cupboards were full of pretty china, and a big, purring cat rummaged in a jar labelled 'Biscuits'.

From outside the library a graceful curved staircase led up to the front half of the house where Natalie had her bed-room and Bobby and then Sam, her third

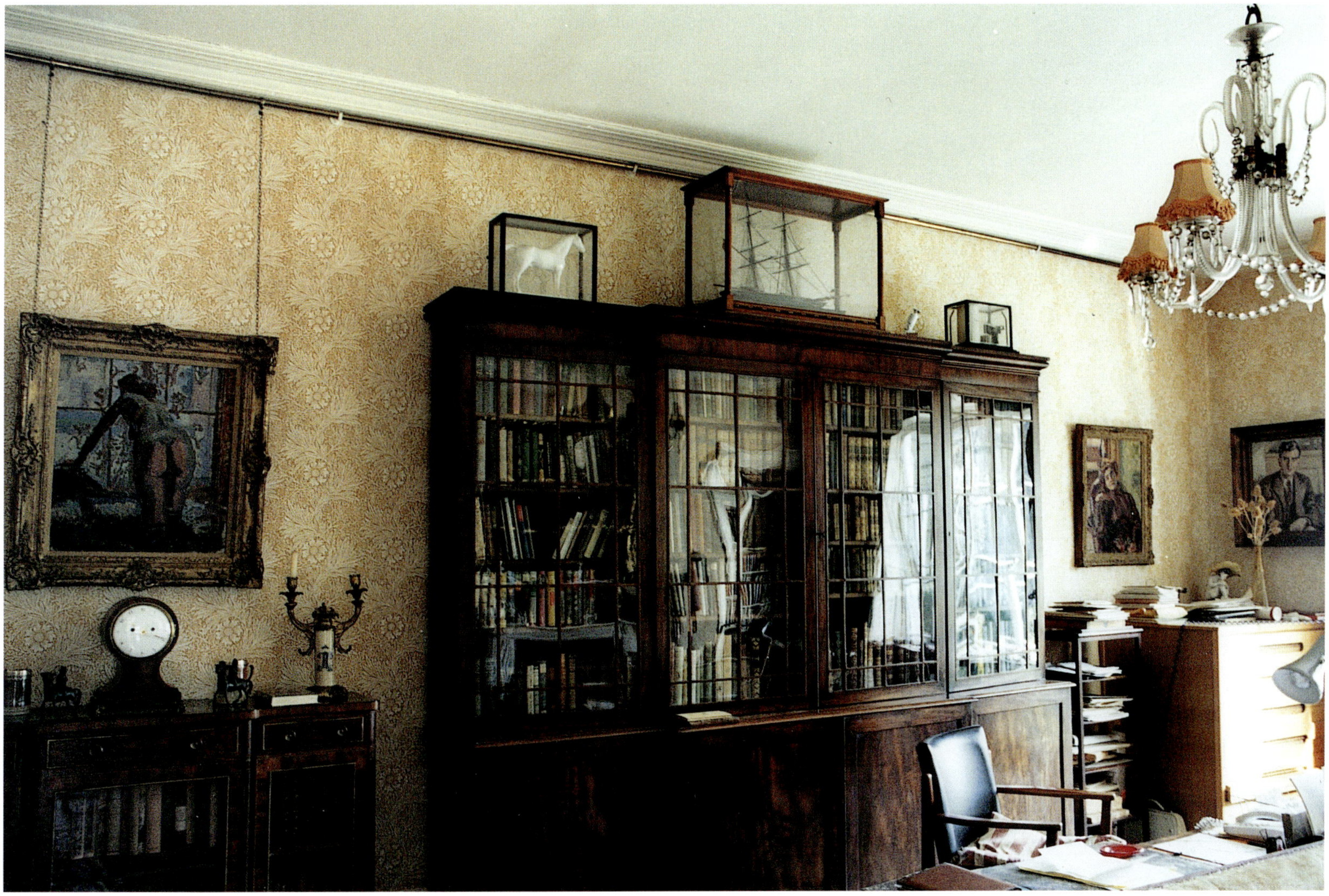

husband, had a dressing-room with a view of the garden and the green fields beyond. Two other bedrooms overlooked the conservatory and kitchen garden. Natalie's large corner bedroom almost reminded one of a dressing-room in a theatre: wonderful exotic garments hanging from doors and the standard lamp, scarves and shawls flung over chairs, hats and flowers and feathers and strings of necklaces draped on lamps and mirrors; but on the walls several exquisite pen and ink drawings by Gilman, a whole group of botanical watercolours by John Nash and quite a few of his humorous drawings. Toulouse-Lautrec's *The Jockey* and the three Paul Gauguin prints hung in Bobby's dressing-room.

There were several more bedrooms at the back of the house, every wall covered with pictures and, through a bathroom, a locked door led to the mysterious Picture Room. This was a racked store where the overflow of paintings, drawings and watercolours by Bevan and other artists were kept, plus the remainder of work from Bobby's mother Stanislawa de Karlowska's studio. These were used for regular re-hangs and to fill in the gaps when pictures were lent to exhibitions. Everybody has a different memory of Boxted, arguing about what was hanging where, but of course the pictures were moved about.

The kitchen was used for cosy dinners,

Fig. 31 · The library at Boxted House with works by Harold Gilman and a portrait of Bobby Bevan by Adrian Daintrey on the walls.

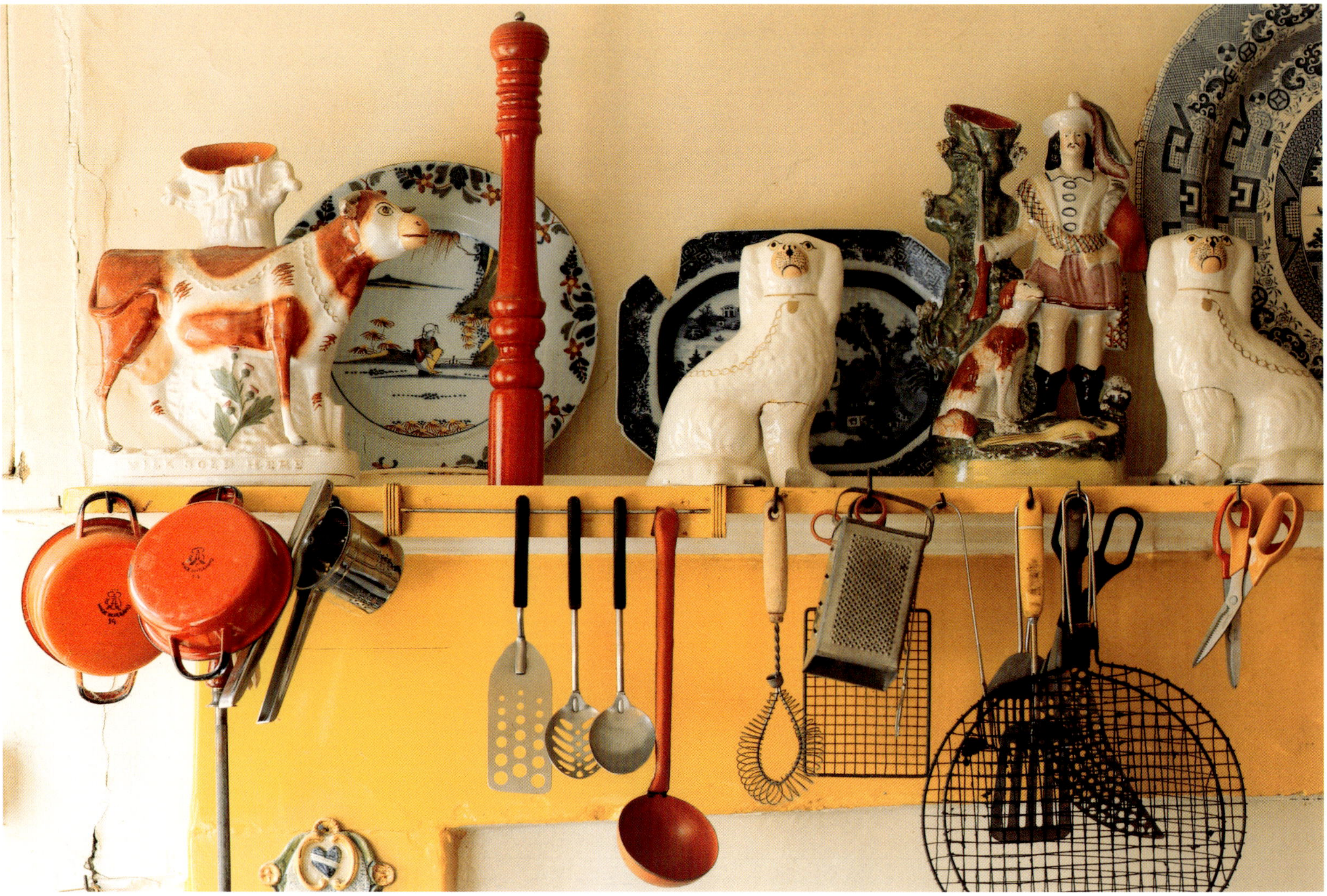

Fig. 32 · A detail of the kitchen in Boxted House.

particularly in winter warmed by the Aga. Natalie was an artistic cook, throwing things together, farmhouse chickens, lots of herbs, tiny new vegetables from the garden, which tasted delicious and looked so pretty, usually eaten off rather rough ceramic shallow bowls, decorated with swimming carp, made by a friend. The dishes and plates, jugs and glasses were all different but very much Bobby's taste and Natalie's personal style, and for years she had collected nineteenth-century Staffordshire figures which stood in groups on shelves, mantelpieces and furniture.

The dining-room, with its yellow Turkey carpet, came into action if there was a house full of people. This was grander stuff, bringing into use a dinner service of late eighteenth-century French porcelain, decorated with a pattern of roses and lots of gilt, the table covered with twinkling glass and Natalie's own sculpture of tumbling clowns lit by candelabra. Out would come wonderful wine from Bobby's cellar. Natalie was an exceptionally welcoming hostess, her high spirits infectious: 'Another little drink, darling?' holding her glass in the air and doing a little dance. She loved dogs and babies and pretty girls. Seeing a pretty girl at a party she would approvingly comment 'Lovely girlie, lovely dress' with one of her irresistible smiles – dazzling, warm, amused and seductive. It was given with the confidence of a great

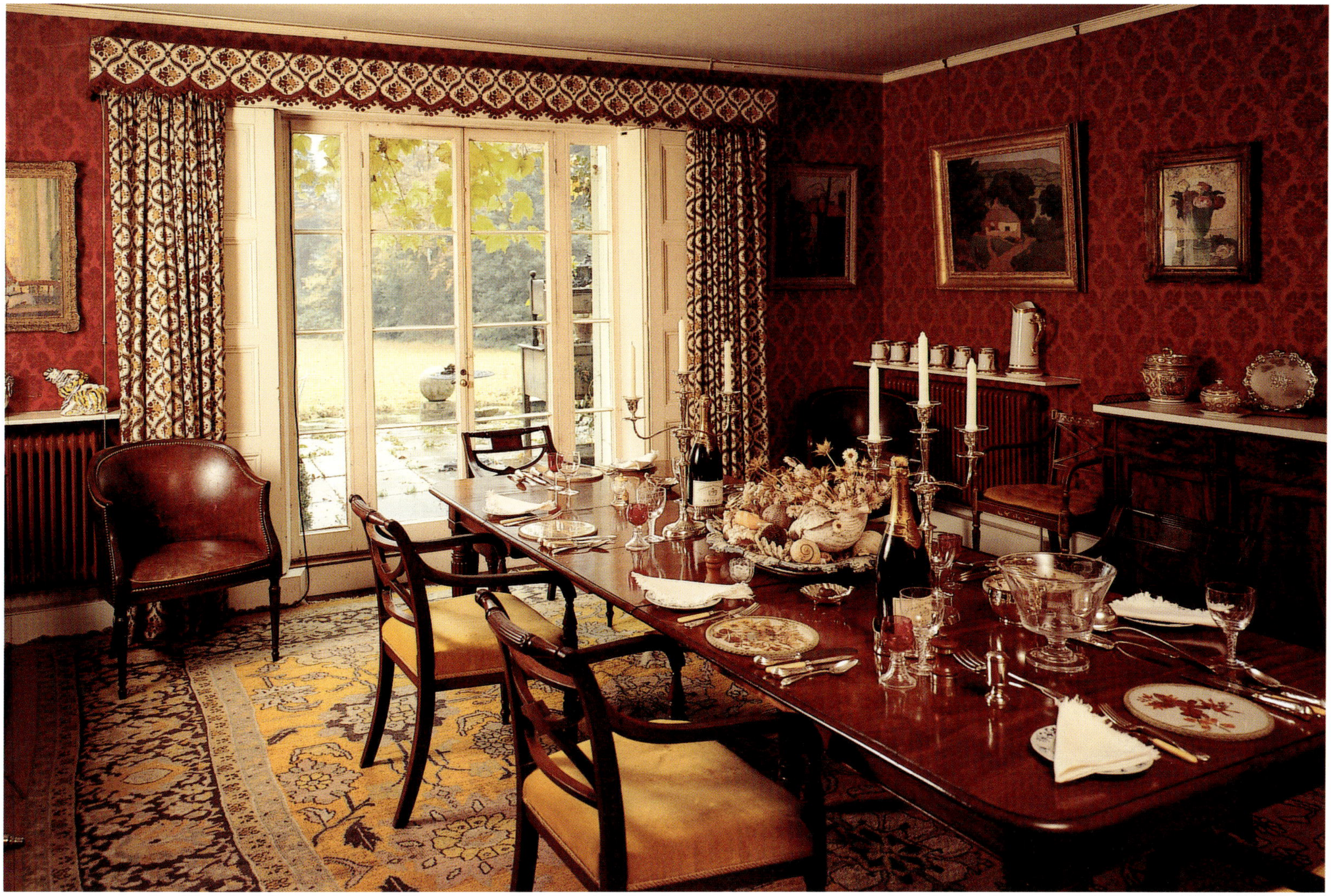

beauty, but with unusual generosity: she was always a participant, never simply an exhibit.

When I first met her in the early 1970s she was easily the most glamorous, most attractive woman in any room. In the evening her clothes were another way of expressing her flamboyant wit, with long coats of Turkish and Indian fabrics, colours and patterns put together as only Natalie could, never overdressed but drawing every eye. Real style, real Bohemian chic. At Boxted she would wear high-necked cream silk shirts under an embroidered waistcoat, a large gold rose at the neck and gold and pearl bunches-of-grapes earrings, fawn-coloured knickerbockers, pale silk stockings showing off shapely legs, and little fawn pumps.

Natalie was the most loving and lovable woman of enormous generosity. She was also a talented painter and sculptor, and artistically creative in everything she did – one recognised her exceptionally beautiful writing on an envelope immediately – but she was totally lacking in pomposity and always ready to laugh. She was fun.

Fig. 33 · The dining-room at Boxted House with works by Harold Gilman, Stanislawa de Karlowska, Robert Bevan and Harry Jonas on the walls, and shell and dried-flower arrangements by Natalie Bevan on the table.

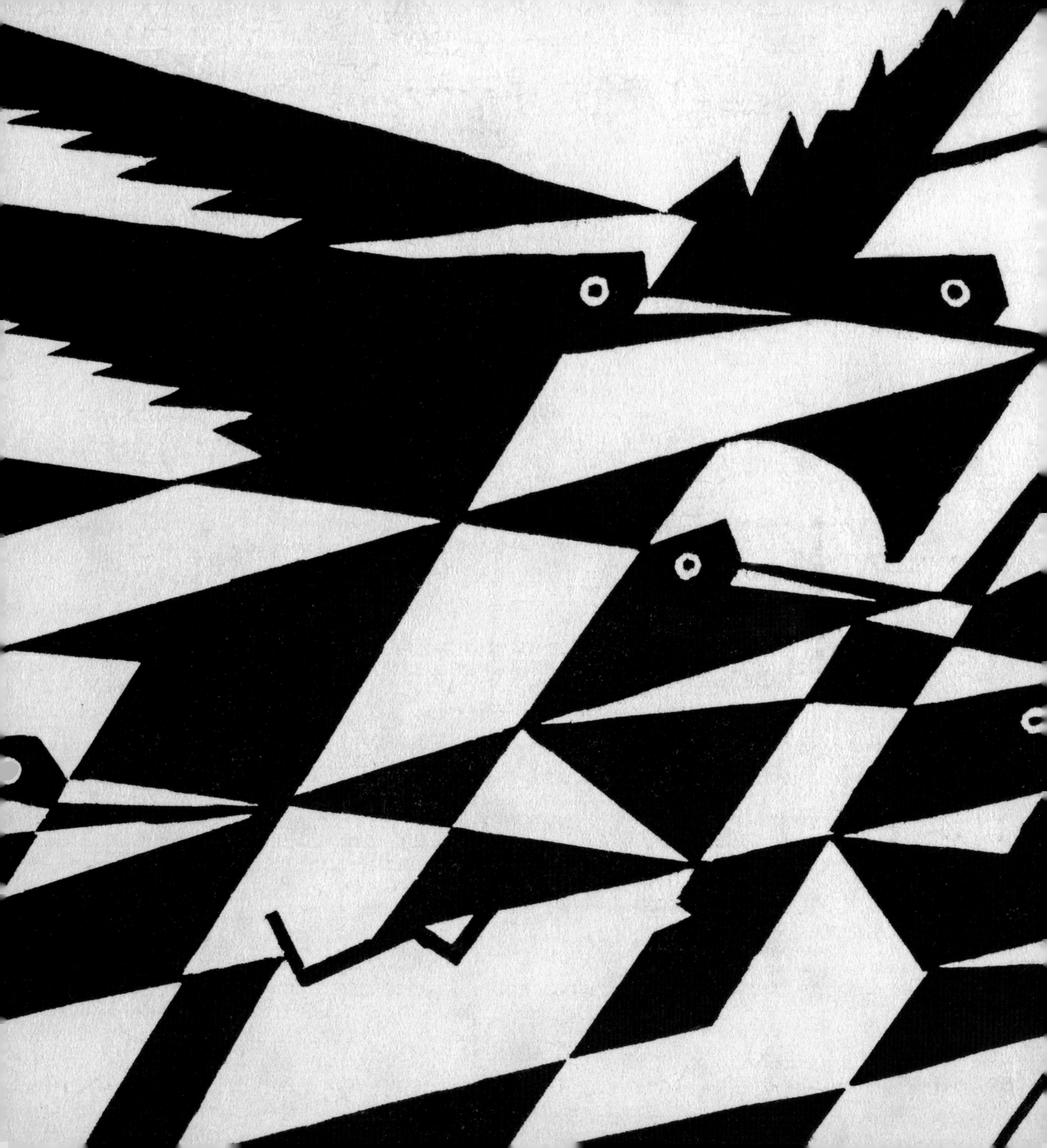

Memories of Bobby Bevan at Bensons

DICK CHAPMAN

Fig. 34· Edward McKnight Kauffer, detail from *Flight*, 1918
Private collection

BOVRIL, Marmite, Colman's mustard, Guinness, Woodbine cigarettes: Bobby Bevan is the unlikely link between these mainstays of early twentieth-century British life and some of the finest British artists of the period.

Advertising must have seemed a strange career choice for the son of wealthy and cultivated parents, who was also the winner of scholarships to Westminster and Christ Church. But he thrived in it and rose to the top. He was not the first Oxford graduate to join what was then London's largest advertising agency, S.H. Benson Ltd. When he started there in 1923, Dorothy L. Sayers had already been there a year. She invented the wildly popular Mustard Club, coined the slogan *My Goodness, My Guinness*, and used Bensons' Kingsway offices as the setting for her first best-seller, *Murder Must Advertise*. Later the firm was joined by another best-selling writer, Julian Yeatman, co-author of *1066 and All That*.

Bobby Bevan remained at Bensons until his retirement in 1964, apart from war service between 1939 and 1945. In 1954 he gave me my first job. Like himself thirty years earlier, I was fresh from Oxford and starting as a trainee copywriter. By then he was the firm's chairman. We were all in awe of him. He was a commanding and imposing presence, with the Churchillian manner adopted by many top businessmen at that time: formidable but with a twinkle. He was never referred to or addressed by name, always as chairman. For any of the staff to call him Bobby was unthinkable. He belonged to a generation that dealt in unadorned surnames. In the directors' corridor he was often heard summoning his secretary, Miss Bone, with the booming monosyllable 'Bone!'

Bobby Bevan operated at the highest level. His office resembled the study of the head of an Oxford college. It was fitted out with magnificent eighteenth-century furniture and hung with many paintings. There he presided over meetings where he would usually, at some stage, reach for a copy pad and revert to his earlier days, scribbling headlines and slogans. He did not claim to have invented the phrase 'Guinness is good for you' but he recalled having to persuade the executives at Guinness that it would not be improved by changing it to 'Guinness is so good for you'.

The paintings that lined the walls of his office and the adjoining corridors looked intriguing to the staff, though none of us knew much about them, except that some were the work of the chairman's father.

Natalie Bevan would come in from time to time and re-arrange them or bring another to be hung. Always calm and elegant, she brought a gracious atmosphere to the rushed and crisis-ridden corridors.

Even in those days, advertising made enormous amounts of money, and the people working in it were well-rewarded. The directors of Bensons 'lived lush', as one of them put it. Bobby Bevan's hobby was ocean-yacht racing, not a pauper's pastime. He had a uniformed chauffeur and a Daimler to convey him from Boxted House to city board rooms, to the Garrick Club and to the Belgravia headquarters of the Institute of Practitioners in Advertising (IPA), the trade association of Britain's advertising agencies, of which he was president. He won his CBE for his work at the IPA. Its mission was to turn the grubby trade of advertising into a respectable profession. It was uphill work. Intellectuals and many others were fond of denigrating it. A short time before, his namesake Aneurin Bevan had castigated advertising as 'An evil growth on an evil society'.

The paintings that Bobby Bevan loved and the work he was so good at seem to have occupied separate sections of his mind. Despite his family background and the work on show in the offices, Bensons under his leadership did nothing to equal the artistic patronage of its close rival Crawfords, with its modernist offices designed by Frederick Etchells and its posters by Edward McKnight-Kauffer. Perhaps this was because in his advertising work Bobby Bevan was always more of a word-man than a picture-man. Also, the mass-market products that Bensons advertised called for more robust illustrators, none more so than Guinness. John Gilroy's famous posters, such as the man carrying a girder on his head, or the toucans, were superb, but definitely in the tradition of commercial rather than fine art.

By the time of Bobby Bevan's retirement in 1964, I had already left Bensons to start a new career outside advertising. But I did later meet the Bevans one last time. It was in 1965, at the Summer Exhibition at the Royal Academy, London. They greeted me warmly, a handsome elderly couple devoting their time to their shared love of the visual arts. The picture-filled galleries seemed their natural habitat. He still had nearly ten years left to live, she more than forty.

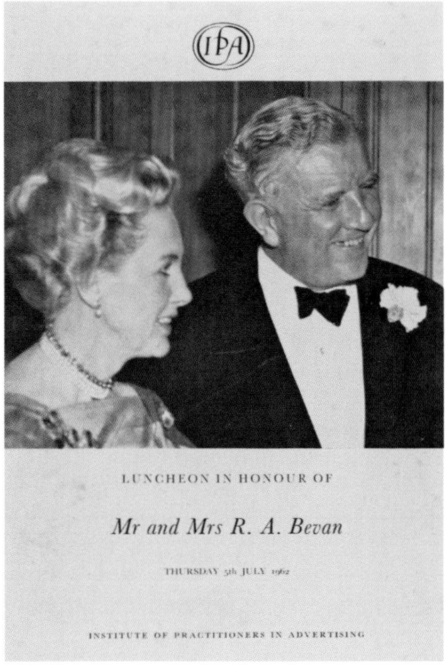

Fig. 35 · Invitation card to a luncheon in honour of Mr and Mrs R.A. Bevan which was held by the Institute of Practitioners in Advertising on 5 July 1962.
Private collection

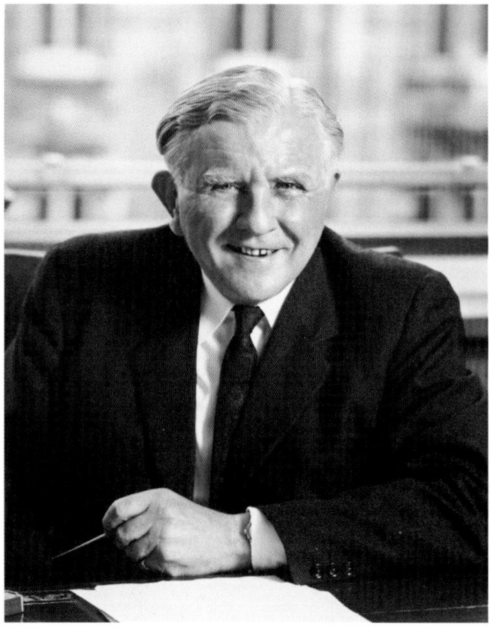

Fig. 36 · Bobby Bevan at S.H. Benson Ltd, London, *c.*1961.
Private collection

Exhibition Checklist

CATALOGUE NOTE

Works with an asterisk ⋆ are illustrated and those marked with a cross + toured to Gainsborough's House, Sudbury. All works are from private collections unless otherwise stated. Works are listed alphabetically under the artist's name and are ordered by medium: works on paper, paintings, sculptures. Dimensions are provided in centimetres, height × width × depth. Sight-sizes are given where actual sizes were unobtainable

JOHN ARMSTRONG 1893–1973

Velocitor, 1930–1 ⋆
Signed with initials lower right: JA
Oil on canvas, 61.2 × 68.8

Abstract Composition, 1933
Signed with initials lower right: JA
Oil on canvas, 68.3 × 51.3

Still Life with Leeks, 1955 +⋆
Oil on canvas, 40.8 × 30.5

Still Life: Pots and Fruit, 1962
Signed and dated lower right: John Armstrong 1962
Oil on canvas, 20.2 × 30.5

RICHARD BEDFORD 1883–1967

Wood Louse, 1950s ⋆
Marble, 13.5 × 22.5 × 18

NATALIE BEVAN 1909–2007

Elephant and Columbine, c.1968 +⋆
Glazed ceramic, 26.5 × 34.5 × 22.4

ROBERT BEVAN 1865–1925

Poplars, c.1892
Lithograph on paper laid on paper, 25.2 × 34.8

Sabot Makers, c.1892 +⋆
Lithograph, 25.5 × 34.5

The Plough, c.1893
Lithograph on buff paper, 25 × 34.7

Peasants at Mass, c.1894
Lithograph on paper laid on paper, 11.8 × 20

Bringing up the Pack on Winsford Hill, 1895
Inscribed along the lower edge: Bringing up The pack on Winsford Hill. / "Hold hard there! Please"! pen and ink on paper, 20.9 × 24 sight size

The Artist's Wife, 1898 +⋆
Lithograph, 23.5 × 18.5 paper 32.2 × 25.5

'The Meet' from 4 Hunting Scenes, 1898–9
Lithograph, 25 × 33.2

'Found!' from 4 Hunting Scenes, 1898–9 +⋆
Lithograph, 25 × 33.5

'The Flying Pack' from 4 Hunting Scenes, 1898–9
Lithograph, 24.8 × 33.3

'Who-o-p!' (first stone) from 4 Hunting Scenes, 1898–9
Lithograph, 24.6 × 33.5

Hay Carts, Cumberland Market, c.1915
With stamped monogram lower right
Crayon on paper, 25.7 × 35.7

Farmstead at Blackdown Hills, 1916
Signed lower left: Robert Bevan
Watercolour and crayon on paper 25.4 × 34.3

Horse Dealers (Ward's Repository no.1), 1919 +⋆
Signed in pencil lower right underneath image: Robert Bevan
Lithograph, 27.6 × 37.5

The Horse Mart (Barbican no.1), 1920 ⋆
Signed in pencil lower left beneath image: Robert P. Bevan
Lithograph, 26.7 × 37.2

Horse Dealers at the Barbican (Barbican no.2), 1921 +
Signed in pencil lower right beneath image: Robert P. Bevan
Lithograph, 29.7 × 35.4

Sale at Ward's Repository (Ward's no.2), 1921
Lithograph, 31 × 36.5

Smithy Barn, Bolham, 1919
Signed in pencil lower right beneath image: Robert P. Bevan
Lithograph, 21.8 × 26.3

The Smithy, Luppitt, 1920
Signed in pencil lower right beneath image: Robert P. Bevan
Lithograph, 23.3 × 30.8

Pub at Luppitt, c.1923 +
Watercolour, crayon and pencil on paper, 26.2 × 33.5 sight-size

Cows and Cowherd, c.1921–2 +
watercolour and crayon on paper, 27.2 × 37.9 sight-size

The Plantation, 1922
Signed in pencil lower right underneath image: Robert P. Bevan
Lithograph, 30.5 × 35.3

A London Church, 1924
Signed in pencil lower right underneath image: Robert P. Bevan
Lithograph, 29.5 × 35

Crocks, 1924–5
Lithograph, 29 × 35.2

The Cottage on the Common, 1925
Crayon and watercolour on paper, 28.3 × 36.5

The Gate at Szeliwy, 1901 +★
Signed lower: Robert Bevan
Oil on canvas, 30.4 × 33.5

Study for 'The Courtyard', c.1904 +★
Signed lower right: R B–N
Oil on board, 24.7 × 30.2

The Small Lake, Poland, 1908
Signed and dated lower left: Robert Bevan 1908
Oil on canvas, 42.3 × 53.4

The Artist's Daughter, c.1908 +★
Oil on board, 33.7 × 24.6

The Cab Yard – Evening, c.1910
Oil on canvas, 63.5 × 76.3

The Front Field at Horsgate, c.1911
Oil on canvas, 46 × 56

Gravelye Farm, Cuckfield, c.1911 +★
Oil on canvas, 65 × 81.4

Evening in the Culme Valley, 1912★
Oil on canvas, 50.8 × 59.7

A Devonshire Valley no.2, c.1913 +★
Oil on canvas, 50.7 × 61.2

Whisky and Soda, 1914
Oil on canvas, 47 × 40

Town Field, Horsgate, c.1914★
Signed lower left: Bevan
Oil on canvas, 38 × 46

Showing at Tattersall's, 1919★
Signed lower left: Robert Bevan
Oil on canvas, 58 × 71
The Ashmolean Museum, Oxford. Presented by R.A. Bevan, the artist's son, 1957.

The Smithy, Luppitt, c.1920★
Signed lower left: Bevan
Oil on canvas, 56 × 66.3

A Polish Church, Mydlow, 1921–2 +★
Oil on canvas, 62.2 × 81.5

Fields at Applehayes, 1922 +
Signed lower left: Bevan
Oil on canvas, 50.8 × 61

Stoneacre Farm no. 2, 1924
Signed lower left: Robert Bevan
Oil on canvas, 50.3 × 61.1

PAUL CÉZANNE 1839–1906

Portrait of Guillaumin with Hanged Man, 1873 +
Etching, 15.3 × 12

GEORGE CLAUSEN 1852–1944

Sharpening a Scythe, c.1893–5 +
Signed with the initials lower left: G C
Pencil on paper, 23.8 × 19.3 sight-size

ADRIAN DAINTREY 1902–1988

Natalie and Bobby on the Terrace, Boxted House, 1957 +★
Signed, dated and inscribed bottom left: Adrian Daintrey 1957 August Boxted
Watercolour and ink on paper, 36.7 × 50.5

EDWARD O'RORKE DICKEY 1894–1977

Embankment Jive, 1920s
Signed in pencil lower right beneath image: EMORDickey
Woodcut on paper, 10 × 12.2

HENRI GAUDIER-BRZESKA 1891–1915

Horse, 1913★
Signed in pencil on card lower right: HenriGaudierBrzeska
Pen and ink on paper laid on card, 25 × 38.5 paper; 40.6 × 55.6 card

Horace Brodzky, c.1913
Ink on paper, 35.6 × 27.2
Anthony d'Offay, London

Nude, 1917–18
Ink on paper, 38.1 × 23.5
Anthony d'Offay, London

Cat, 1913 +
Moulded earthenware with ceramic glaze and Omega stamp, 11.6 × 13 × 7.8
Anthony d'Offay, London

Ornament, 1914 +★
Animal bone, 17.1 long
Anthony d'Offay, London

PAUL GAUGUIN 1848–1906

Two Tahitian Girls, 1894 +★
Inscribed, signed and dated lower right: à l'ami Baven / P G o ‹ 1894 ‹
Monotype, 19 × 16.5

MARK GERTLER 1891–1939

Portrait of the Artist's Mother, 1924 +★
Signed and dated upper left: Mark Gertler / 1924
Oil on canvas, 76.5 × 70.5

Supper (Natalie Denny), 1928 +★
Oil on canvas, 106.8 × 71.2

HAROLD GILMAN 1876–1919

Mother and Child, 1918
Signed lower right: Gilman
Pen, ink and chalk on paper, 29.2 × 22.8

Portrait of Spencer Gore, c.1911–12★
Oil on cardboard, 38 × 32

Madeleine Knox, 1910–11 +★
Signed lower right: H. Gilman
Oil on canvas, 61 × 45.5

Nude at a Window, c.1912★
Signed lower right: H. Gilman
Oil on canvas, 61 × 50.8

Portrait of Old Lady, 1911–12
Oil on canvas, 40.8 × 30.5

Mrs Robert Bevan, c.1913 +★
Signed lower left: H. Gilman
Oil on canvas, 61.1 × 45.7

CHARLES GINNER 1878–1952

La Vieille Balayeuse, Dieppe, 1913★
Signed lower right: C. Ginner
Oil on canvas, 63 × 47

FREDERICK GORE B.1913

Looking Towards the Aegean Sea from the Greek Island of Aegina, 1988 +★
Signed and dated lower right: F. Gore 88.
Oil on canvas, 73.6 × 94.5

SPENCER GORE 1878–1914

Conversation Piece and Self-portrait, c.1910 +
Inscribed lower right: S. F. G.
Oil on board, 32 × 38

FRANCISCO DE GOYA 1746–1828

'The Agility and Audacity of Juanito Apinani in the Ring at Madrid', plate 20 of *La Tauromaquia*, 1816 +★
Etching and aquatint on paper, 24.5 × 35.2 paper 33 × 49

LETT HAINES 1894–1978

Piscatorial, 1931 +★
Signed and dated lower left: Lett 1931
Watercolour, chalk, ink and pencil on paper, 51.3 × 67.2

WENCESLAUS HOLLAR 1607–1677

London, Viewed from Milford Stairs, c.1644
Etching on paper laid on paper, 9.4 × 17.1

A Group of Muffs, 1647
Etching on paper laid on paper, 10.7 × 20.4

Muscarum Scarabeorum, Vermiumque Variae Figure & Formae…, 1646
Etching on paper laid on paper, 7.9 × 12

AUGUSTUS JOHN 1878–1961

Wyndham Lewis, c.1903 +
Etching and drypoint, 17.3 × 14

STANISLAWA DE KARLOWSKA 1876–1952

'Autumn' from The Seasons, 1920s +
Woodcut, 12.7 × 9.5

The Stable Field, Horsgate, c.1914 +★
Signed lower right: S. de Karlowska
Oil on canvas, 46.5 × 38.5

Backs of Houses, Percy Street, c.1919★
Signed lower right: S de Karlowska
Oil on canvas, 61.2 × 51.0

EDWARD MCKNIGHT KAUFFER 1890–1954

Flight, 1918★
Signed and dated in pencil lower right: E. McKnight Kauffer 1918
Woodcut, 13.5 × 22.5

HENRY LAMB 1883–1960

Head of a Boy, c.1910
Inscribed lower right: Julien
Pencil on paper, 25.1 × 20 sight-size

CEDRIC MORRIS 1889–1982

Paysage du Jardin no.2, 1931 +★
Signed and dated lower left: CEDRIC MORRIS 31
Oil on canvas, 71.2 × 63.6

The Blue Poppy, 1932★
Signed and dated lower left: CEDRIC MORRIS 32
Oil on canvas, 76 × 63.5

JOHN NASH 1893–1977

The Threshing Machine, 1914★
Signed and dated lower right: JOHN NASH / 1914
Watercolour, chalk, ink and pencil on paper, 42.3 × 56 sight-size

Bristol Docks, c.1927
Signed lower right: John Nash
Watercolour and pencil, 30.2 × 37.5 sight-size

Girls being Tiresome, 1965 +★
Signed and inscribed lower right: Girls being Tiresome / JN. / Mundesly on Sea
Inscribed on backboard: Mundlesey on Sea / Norfolk / 1965
Watercolour and pen and ink on paper, 12.3 × 14.4 sight-size

Banter, c.1925
Signed and inscribed lower left: "Banter" / John Nash.
Pen and ink and pencil on paper, 23.5 × 14.2 sight-size

Ice and Snow, 1959 +★
Signed lower left: John Nash
Oil on canvas, 63.5 × 76.3

PAUL NASH 1889–1946

Tree Group, 1919
Signed in pencil lower right beneath image: Paul Nash
Wood engraving, 9.5 × 7

Elms, 1919–20
Inscribed in pencil upper left above image: Mr Bevan
Inscribed lower right under image: Paul Nash
Wood engraving, 9.5 × 5.7

CHRISTOPHER R.W. NEVINSON 1889–1946

Broadway Girls, c.1919★
Signed lower left: C. R. W. Nevinson
Pastel on board, 19 × 25

The Lilies of the Café, c.1919 +★
Pastel on paper, 63.5 × 45.8

DENZIL REEVES B.1926

Boxted House, c.1958 +★
Woodcut, 9.7 × 14.2 oval

WILLIAM ROBERTS 1895–1980

Boozers, c.1925
Signed in pencil lower left beneath image: William Roberts
Etching on paper, 9.7 × 9.7

WALTER SICKERT 1860–1942

The Old Middlesex (the large plate), 1910
etching, 23.8 × 30.6

That Old-Fashioned Mother of Mine, 1928 +
Etching and engraving, 19.5 × 14.8

Cheerio, 1929 +
Etching, 18 × 13.7

The System, 1924–8 +★
Signed lower left: Sickert A.R.A.
Oil on linen on canvas, 61.2 × 38.8

JOHN SKEAPING 1901–1980

Gazelle, 1928
Alabaster, 30.4 long

THÉOPHILE-ALEXANDRE STEINLEN 1859–1923

Tramway Interior, 1896
Lithograph, 26 × 34.3

HENRI DE TOULOUSE-LAUTREC 1864–1901

Divan Japonais, 1892–3★
Colour lithograph, 80.6 × 62.1

The Jockey, 1899 +
Colour lithograph, 50.8 × 34.9

FRANCIS UNWIN 1885–1925

Reaping and Binding, 1917 +
Etching, 6.8 × 16.8

Hampstead, 1919
Signed in pencil lower centre beneath image: – Francis Unwin –
Lithograph, 21 × 33.5

EDOUARD VUILLARD 1868–1940

Siesta (Convalescence), 1893 +
Colour lithograph, 35.2 × 25.2 sight-size

Select Bibliography

Primary Source Material

Colchester Art Society Archive, see www.colchester-artsociety.co.uk

The History of Advertising Trust Archive, see www.hatads.org.uk

The Victor Batte-Lay Trust Archive, see www.theminories.co.uk

Tate Archive, Robert Polhill Bevan Archive (TGA 9210) and Stanislawa de Karlowska Archive (TGA 9216)

Secondary Literature

BARON 2000
Wendy Baron, *Perfect Moderns: A History of the Camden Town Group*, Ashgate Publishing Ltd, Aldershot, 2000

BEVAN 1965
Robert Alexander Bevan, *Robert Bevan 1865–1925: A Memoir by his Son*, Studio Vista, London, 1965

COLCHESTER 1975
The R. A. Bevan Collection, exh. cat., the Minories, Colchester, 1975

COLLINS 1990
Ian Collins, *A Broad Canvas: Art in East Anglia since 1880*, Parke Sutton Publishing, Norwich, 1990

DRY 1968
Graham Dry, *Catalogue Raisonné of the Lithographs and other Prints of Robert Bevan*, Maltzhan Gallery, London, 1968

LONDON 1975
English Paintings from The Bevan Collection, exh. cat., Anthony d'Offay, London, 1975

REYNOLDS AND GRACE 2002
Gwynneth [*sic*] Reynolds and Diana Grace(eds.), *Benton End Remembered: Cedric Morris, Arthur Lett-Haines and the East Anglian School of Painting and Drawing*, Unicorn Press, London, 2002

ROSS 2003
Cathy Ross, *Twenties London: A City in the Jazz Age*, Philip Wilson Publishers, London, 2003

SAYERS 1933
Dorothy L. Sayers, *Murder Must Advertise*, Victor Gollanz Ltd, London, 1933

STENLAKE 1999
Frances Stenlake, *From Cuckfield to Camden Town: The Story of Artist Robert Bevan (1865–1925)*, Cuckfield Museum, Cuckfield, 1999

STENLAKE 2008
Frances Stenlake, *Robert Bevan, from Gauguin to Camden Town*, Unicorn Press, London, 2008

STRANG 2007
Alice Strang, 'Obituary of Natalie Bevan', *The Independent*, 29 August 2007

SUDBURY 1978
The Bevan Collection, exh. cat., Gainsborough's House, Sudbury, 1978

TUFNELL 2002
Ben Tufnell, *Cedric Morris and Lett Haines: Teaching Art and Life*, Norfolk Museums & Archaeology Service and National Museums & Galleries of Wales, 2003

UPSTONE 2008
Robert Upstone, *Modern Painters: The Camden Town Group*, Tate, London, 2008

Notes

Bobby and Natalie Bevan and the Art at Boxted House Alice Strang

Much of the information about Bobby and Natalie Bevan and Boxted House contained in this essay was provided by Anthea Sieveking and Alan Stewart, in conversation with the author, over a two-year period, from 2006 to 2008.

1. Ronald Blythe, unpublished recollection of Boxted House, 2007, Scottish National Gallery of Modern Art Archive.
2. Bobby was a founder-member and eventual president of the Institute of Practitioners in Advertising (1961–2), during which time he was a founding member of the Advertising Standards Agency. He served as the UK representative on the United Nations Committee on public information and was a member of the Board of Trade's Export Publicity Council. He sat on the Advisory Council on Middle East Trade and was convenor of the council's publicity panel. He was president of the National Advertising Benevolent Society. In 1963 he was awarded the CBE for services in furthering British exports. On his death, Bobby was described in *The Times* as 'the personification of the greatest days of British advertising'. (R.D. Bloomfield, 'Mr R.A. Bevan', *The Times*, 7 January 1975. Information supplied by Ian Lowe in a letter to the author, 11 August 2007).
3. *Natalie Bevan's Circus: Ceramic Figures & Animals*, Anthony d'Offay Fine Art, London, 1968.
4. Undated handwritten letter from Bobbie [*sic*] Bevan to Miss Natalie Denny, envelope post-marked 16 February 1928, private collection.
5. Letter from Mark Gertler to Marjorie Hodgkinson dated 29 February 1928, quoted in Noel Carrington(ed.), *Mark Gertler: Selected Letters*, London 1965, p.226. We are grateful to Sarah MacDougall for drawing our attention to

this letter and for providing further information about the paintings by Gertler at Boxted House in a letter to Caroline Cuthbert of 3 July 2007 and an e-mail to the author, 14 August 2007.

6. This date appears on napkins, printed to mark the occasion, which remain in the Sieveking family. This contradicts Lance Sieveking, who in his autobiography, *The Eye of the Beholder*, London, 1957, p.300, gives their wedding date as 6 October 1928.
7. For a short period at the start of World War Two, Bobby was director of General Production at the Ministry of Information, before joining the Navy with whom he saw active service. Towards the end of the war he was appointed as a captain RNVR to Washington. In 1941 he was awarded the OBE for military services. See 'Obituary of Mr R.A. Bevan', *The Times*, 20 December 1974.
8. Undated typescript of the opening speech given by Bobby Bevan at *The Camden Town Group* exhibition at the Cecil Higgins Art Gallery, Bedford, 3 October – 2 November 1969, private collection.
9. The Bevan Gift, of 1957, to the Ashmolean Museum, Oxford, was made in memory of Robert Polhill Bevan. It consisted of nine paintings, including four by Bevan, four drawings, twenty-seven sketchbooks and eighteen lithographs by Bevan, two drawings by Harold Gilman, one drawing each by Charles Ginner, Spencer Gore and John Nash, and a print by Malcolm Drummond. Bobby later gave two drawings by his father and two paintings by his mother to the museum. The purchase fund he established in 1957 was used to acquire a painting by Bevan and one by Gilman, nineteen drawings including five by Gilman, four each by Walter Sickert and Maxwell Gordon Lightfoot, two by Henry Lamb and single examples by Gore, Wyndham Lewis, J.B. Manson and William Ratcliffe. Information compiled by Ian Lowe 12 April 1975 and supplied to the author on 11 August 2007.
10. As noted by Ginner in the back of the first of his manuscript notebooks in the Tate Archive (TGA 9319.1), calling Bevan's painting 'Sussex Landscape'. Information supplied by Wendy Baron in an e-mail to the author on 4 January 2008. A Mayor Gallery receipt for the purchase of Walter Sickert's painting, *The System* dated 30 January 1951 is in the Tate Archive (TGA 9210.1.5).
11. Recalled by E.M. O'Rorke Dickey in Colchester 1975, unpaginated.
12. Thanks are due to Professor Andrew Causey for dating this and other works by Gilman which hung at Boxted House, in an e-mail to the author, 1 February 2008.
13. See *Harold Gilman*, exh. cat., the Minories, Colchester, March 1969, cat. no.32. Bobby is likely to have purchased Gilman's *Mrs Robert Bevan* of *c.*1913 from the artist's exhibition at the Reid Gallery, London of 1964 (cat. no.22). This fact pointed out by Wendy Baron, see note 10. Gilman painted three portraits of Karlowska, all of which Bobby acquired on the art market, at different times, after the artist's death, as stated in *Harold Gilman*, exh. cat., Arts Council of Great Britain touring exhibition, 1981–2, cat. no.45.
14. See Evelyn Silber, *Gaudier-Brzeska: Life and Art*, London, 1996, no.101, p.274.
15. Undated handwritten addendum to handwritten letter dated 1 January 1915 from Henri Gaudier to Mrs Stanislawa Bevan, private collection.
16. Undated handwritten recollection of her friendship with the artist John Armstrong by Natalie Bevan, private collection, quoted in part in the Foreword in, *John Armstrong: Paintings 1935–1970*, exh. cat., the Minories, Colchester, 1977.
17. Handwritten letter dated 13 January 1928 from Mark Gertler to Miss Natalie Denny, private collection.
18. Sayers 1933.
19. Anthony Powell, 'Messengers of Day', in *To Keep the Ball Rolling*, vol.2, London, 1978, pp.33–4.
20. We are grateful to Armstrong's widow, Annette Armstrong, for providing information about these paintings and her husband's relationship with the Bevans, in a letter to the author of 9 January 2008.
21. Natalie Bevan, 'The Perfect Day', *The Sunday Times*, 1 January 1967, p.22.
22. We are grateful to Christopher Martin, Assistant Librarian, University of Portsmouth Library for providing information about these works in an e-mail, 17 January 2008, and a letter to the author, 22 January 2008.
23. For example, Lance Sieveking's book, *Dressing Gowns and Glue*, London, 1919, was illustrated by John Nash and edited by Paul Nash.
24. Natalie Bevan quoted in John Rothenstein, *John Nash*, London, 1983, p.92.
25. As quoted in John Rothenstein, Ibid., p.82.
26. See *Exhibition of Paintings and Drawings by John Nash CBE RA*, exh. cat., The Royal Academy of Arts, London, 1967. John Nash, *The Lake at Boxted House*, Chelmsford and Essex Museum, accession no.1971.235.
27. Bobby's salary from Bensons allowed him to start making modest acquisitions in the early 1930s, often from the Leicester Galleries in London. The ambition of his purchases grew after World War Two in line with his increasing income.
28. See Reynolds and Grace 2002, and Tufnell 2003.
29. See *Cedric Morris Retrospective*, exh. cat., National Museum of Wales, Cardiff, 1968, cat. nos. 54 and 68 and *Cedric Morris*, exh. cat., Tate

Gallery, London, May 1984, cat. no.84. Bobby acquired important works for Bensons by other artists, including John Nash and Mark Gertler, whose *Portrait of the Artist's Mother* of 1924 was given back to Bobby on his retirement. Bobby's friend the typographer John Lewis recalled Bobby asking him to install a permanent exhibition on the history of printing in the corridors of Bensons. See John Lewis, *Such Things Happen: The Life of a Typographer*, Stowmarket, 1994, p.170.

30. Bobby was also a member of the council of the Byam Shaw School of Drawing and Painting, London, a chairman of the New Art Centre, London and a vice-president of the Friends of the Ashmolean. Thanks are due to Frances Stenlake and Ian Lowe for providing this information in an e-mail to the author of 27 June 2007 and a letter to the author of 11 August 2007 respectively. Bobby was also a member of the Ministry of Education's National Advisory Council on Art Education. See 'Obituary of Mr R.A. Bevan', see note 7.
31. Information provided by Alan Ellis of Colchester Art Society in letters to the author, 8 and 18 January 2008.
32. Thanks are due to Anthony Atkinson for information about Colchester Art School provided in a telephone conversation with the author on 19 January 2008.
33. See Graham Reynolds, 'Foreword', in Sudbury 1978, unpaginated.
34. Ronald Blythe, see note 1.
35. On Bobby's commission, Edward Ardizzone illustrated *Game Pie*, by Stanley Penn and John Trench, published by Bensons' client, Guinness, in 1955. See Brian Selby, *The Book of Guinness Advertising*, London, 1985, p.221. Information supplied by The History of Advertising Trust Archive to the author on 18 January 2008. See John Lewis, note 29. Bobby was a co-owner of the ocean-racing yacht *Phryna*, a member of the Royal Ocean Racing Club and a founder member of the Board of Governors of the *Cutty Sark*. This information supplied by Frances Stenlake, see note 30.
36. Maggi Hambling, unpublished recollection of Boxted House, 2007, Scottish National Gallery of Modern Art Archive.
37. Bobby discussed his youthful ideas of becoming an architect with Raymond Erith, but decided to enter a more lucrative profession having been party to his parents' financial struggles. As reported to the author by Erith's daughter, Lucy Archer, in a telephone conversation of 13 January 2008.
38. Anthony Powell, *A Dance to the Music of Time*, in twelve volumes published by Heinemann, London, between 1951 and 1975.
39. See Lance Sieveking, note 6, p.299.
40. See Frances Stenlake's essay in this publication for further details.
41. See Anthony d'Offay, 'Introduction', in London 1975, unpaginated.
42. Frederick Gore, unpublished recollection of Boxted House, 2007, Scottish National Gallery of Modern Art Archive.
43. Frederick Gore, Ibid.
44. Minories, see note 11; d'Offay, see note 41, and *An Exhibition of The Bevan Gift of Paintings and Drawings by The Camden Town Group*, exh. cat., the Ashmolean Museum, Oxford, 1975.
45. Sudbury 1978, see note 33.

Bevan is Good for You Frances Stenlake

1. Mrs R.P. Bevan correspondence, Tate Archive 9210/1/4.
2. R.A. Bevan correspondence, Tate Archive 9210/1/5.
3. Ibid.
4. Ibid.
5. F. Gordon Roe, 'The Adventurous Robert Bevan', *The British Racehorse*, July 1958, pp.114–20. See also William Gaunt, 'Robert Bevan', *The British Racehorse*, December 1970, pp.569–75.
6. *The Connoisseur*, vol.158, April 1965, pp.244–8.